750

OKLAHOMA **TRACKMAKER** SERIES

OKLAHOMA TRACKMAKER SERIES

L. E. PHILLIPS

L. E. Phillips

L. E. PHILLIPS

BANKER, OIL MAN, CIVIC LEADER

by Billy M. Jones

Kenny A. Franks, Series Editor

 Published for the Oklahoma Heritage Association
by Western Heritage Books, Inc.

ISBN: 0-86546-016-7

For the daughters I never had—
whom my sons were smart enough to marry.

Tammy, Pam, and Debbie

PREFACE

This is the life story of Lee Eldas Phillips. He, along with his brother Frank, co-founded the Phillips Petroleum Company of Bartlesville, Oklahoma, in 1917. His biography is a tale of unusual accomplishments and enviable successes, his business experiences a textbook for erstwhile entrepreneurs—a study of failure and achievement, of risk taking and innovation, in a highly competitive, free-market environment.

He was a native Iowan, born near Conway in 1876, the second son of ten children reared by God-fearing Midwestern pioneers. His hard-working parents loved him, but they lived ascetic lives and could provide no more than a meager, agrarian existence in a small rural community. Moreover, his education was barely adequate, his health not always good, and his earliest venture into an owner-manager business enterprise not so successful. And although he developed his talents through determined study and a driving ambition to better himself, his early life nonetheless was one of near poverty and adversity.

"Nearly all men can stand adversity," Abraham Lincoln once said, "but if you want to test a man's character, give him power." Adversity actually was an important factor in shaping Lee Eldas Phillips' will to succeed. Despite the fact that he learned the value of hard work, honesty, and respect for his agrarian heritage, he helped charter in his boyhood years the "Never Sweat Club," a quasi-fraternity composed of the sons of area agriculturalists who swore never again to work as farmers once they reached majority. And Lee pledged to himself a x / L. E. PHILLIPS

few years later not to be destitute or devoid of financial
security once he reached retirement age. Thus adversity
drove him to climb out of the furrows and walk along
a path which progressively marked·him for greatness—
and ultimately brought him into positions of immense
power, both as a nationally-known banker and as an
internationally prominent oilman.

But power was something that rested comfortably
on the shoulders of Lee Eldas Phillips. Adversity had
not embittered him; rather it had conditioned him to
appreciate the good things which came to him. Instead
of trying to rise above his heritage and those who were
less fortunate, he proved a man of genuine character
who cared about his family and friends, one to whom
trusting contemporaries went repeatedly for dependable leadership in shaping the destiny and improving the
quality of life in Bartlesville and in Oklahoma. He never
lost his respect for his humble heritage, never lost his
appreciation for the fundamental, conservative lessons
his family taught him, and never lavishly spent the
wealth he accumulated. He always honored his God and
his country. He was a true patriot and an avid devotee
of the American private enterprise system.

That was the tenor of his character. He was not one
to seek excessive visibility, always rejoicing when his
older brother Frank received recognition for his leadership of Phillips Petroleum or accolades for one of the
company's many accomplishments. Frank knew, as did
those who really counted, that L. E.'s contributions as
co-founder of the company were immense and virtually
incalculable. That was recognition and praise enough
for Lee Eldas Phillips.

Recognition and praise may not suffice to repay the
tremendous debts which the author has incurred in writing this biography. Foremost among them is to Philip
Rex Phillips, eldest son of Lee Eldas, who gave generously of his time and extensive knowledge and who pro-

vided a well-organized array of collected data without which the complete story could not have been told. Others also have been of great help. Former Phillips president Paul Endacott, wise in his perceptions and recollections, provided excellent descriptions of what the early days in the oil fields were like as well as some of Phillips Petroleum's early developmental problems. L. E. Fitzgarrald, a long-time ranking official in the company, proved an invaluable source for understanding some of the functions and interrelationships within the firm. Also Ms. Dorothy Saunders, secretary to both L. E. Phillips and his son, Philip Rex, gave unselfishly of her time and her professional knowledge. And Charles Cummings provided valuable insights into the personal side of L. E. Phillips' management style, as did Glenroy Billbe. To all of these fine people, my genuine thanks for sitting through rather lengthy interview processes.

Kenneth Childers, Vice President for Public Relations, and Robert Finney, Director of the Phillips Petroleum Company Archives, were most encouraging and helpful by making available valuable resource materials, as was Ms. Sandy Smith at the Oklahoma Historical Society Library in Oklahoma City. Thanks also must go to the libraries at the University of Texas at Austin, the University of Oklahoma, and Wichita State University for help in locating some elusive references.

Finally, the author acknowledges his great debt to his colleagues in the College of Business at Wichita State University for their faith and support, to Professor Fran Jabara, the founder and director of the Center for Entrepreneurship and Small Business Management at WSU, and to an intelligent and indefatigable associate, Mrs. Kathlyn Baldwin, who helped in finalizing and typing the manuscript.

Wichita, Kansas   Billy M. Jones
December, 1980

CONTENTS

ILLUSTRATIONS

L. E. PHILLIPS

1

HOME IN IOWA

On April 4, 1905, in the Indian Territory near present Bartlesville, Lee Eldas Phillips, a homesick young Iowan, sat down to write a friend. As he wrote in the graceful penmanship so characteristic of his day, his words were punctuated by the realization that the postal service was "not closely connected" with wilderness Oklahoma. He had begun his trip, along with his older brother Frank, in late February and had received but two letters from his wife, to whom he had been married only two years. Jokingly he wrote his friend, "If you should see the 'misses' tell her I will cut off her allowance if she don't write me." Understandably he was anxious to know about conditions at home and especially about his young son.

In his letter he described the conditions in his Bartlesville setting. It was cold, but perhaps not as cold as Iowa. Roads were terrible, and all streams had to be forded because there were no bridges. The land was so rocky that "a respectful white bean would refuse to grow" on it. But the town was a beehive of activity. Derricks and crude buildings were crowded in unplanned disarray. Oilmen, speculators, and field hands were everywhere, living in whatever accommodations could be found. There was quite a mixture of people, many from the eastern states and England. Two young Englishmen, fresh from London and representing an English Syndicate, told of bringing in a well that was producing 1500 barrels of oil per day. Reflecting a moment, the young Iowan wrote, "If we should get one as good, I fear I would drop dead."[1]

Lee Eldas Phillips was experiencing his second trip to the Indian Territory "to look after his interests in the big oil fields of that section." His older brother Frank had made prior exploratory visits to the area, and had arranged lease rights for several hundred acres of land. Now together, they located a room in that thriving town which they used "as an office and sleeping room combined." A driller was engaged and a well begun.

"Our holdings here look very good," L. E. wrote his friend, "and I feel very sanguine of the outcome. However, it is all a speculation, and to fully appreciate a good well here they say you must first have a dry hole or two." Such was to be his experience. The first effort was marginally productive and had to be abandoned. A second and third attempt resulted in dry holes, more than enough failure "to fully appreciate a good well." Undaunted—and with but sufficient money to make a fourth try—they began drilling the now famous Anna Anderson No. 1. On September 6, 1905, L. E. and Frank Phillips rejoiced with full appreciation when a 250-barrel-a-day gusher blew in.[2]

Little did the brothers know that they stood on the threshold of wealth, power, and greatness, that within a dozen years they would found the Phillips Petroleum Company. They were typical entrepreneurs, thrilled by the early success of their risk taking and determined to risk again whatever assets accrued from Anna Anderson No. 1. They could not know that an unbroken chain of successful wells would reach an unbelievable 81 before they again would drill a dry hole. And they could not visualize the greatness they would bring to Oklahoma, the nation, and the world by developing the oil company that would bear their name.[3]

None of the affluence that Lee Eldas Phillips one day would enjoy was visible when he was born in rural

Conway, Iowa, on August 18, 1876. Indeed, his parents, Lewis Franklin Phillips and Lucinda Josephine Faucett, were hard-working, God-fearing, Midwestern pioneers whose agrarian existence was Spartan even at best. As Lee Eldas, or "L. E." as he was most frequently called, reflected in later years, "We had to work in order to have food, shelter, and clothing."[4] Such was the lot of most of their neighbors, but it was a good life, a life of toil, to be sure, but one well-rounded with meaningful activities, loving families, and faithful friends.

From the time Dr. Henry B. Liggett first spanked his bottom, L. E. had much to be proud of. His ancestry reached back to 1620 when English-born Miles Standish arrived in America aboard the *Mayflower*. Marrilla Standish, a descendant of Miles Standish, was married in December of 1838 in Potter County, Pennsylvania, to Daniel Phillips, whose father had migrated from Wales in the late 18th Century. This marriage united two families of character and heritage. In the jargon of the day they were referred to as "quality folk." The Standish family was known for "even temper, honesty, and temperate habits," none of whom ever used tobacco or intoxicants. Of the earlier Phillips, not much was recorded, but Daniel obviously came from a line of hard-working, resolute, and religious Welshmen. During his early life, he was a "hardy lumberman" and raftsman on the Ohio and Mississippi rivers. After his marriage to Marrilla, he became a farmer and was active in the Dunkers Church, a religion "very much like the Quakers."[5]

Daniel and Marrilla first settled in Meigs County, Ohio, then moved in 1847 to Conway in Jackson County, Iowa—a pattern of migration followed by countless native and newly-arrived Americans in the mid-1800s. Eight children were the result of this union, Lewis Franklin the third child and first son, born on January 4, 1844. He was a "promising child and a great favorite with his (maternal) grandfather Standish."[6]

Sometime in 1855, Daniel moved his family to Stones County, Iowa, where Lewis matured, attended school, and became a carpenter. In 1861, Lewis volunteered for army service in the Second Iowa Battery as a Union soldier and participated in several campaigns, including the seiges of Vicksburg and Nashville. He fought bravely, twice refusing to surrender at Corinth and Tupelo. He was wounded in the arm but not seriously, but emerged from service in 1865 with a serious hearing impairment owing in all likelihood to his duties as a canoneer.

Returning to his Iowa home, he resumed his life as a farmer/carpenter. Soon the handsome L. F. met Lucinda Josephine Faucett, "the most beautiful girl in his section" of Iowa. He courted and won her hand, and they were married in Des Moines, Iowa, on July 3, 1867. Lucinda, "Josie" as she was called, was the daughter of Reverend Thomas Linch Faucett and Mary Jane Tate. She was the second of 12 children born to the deeply religious couple. A blacksmith by profession, Thomas had helped build the first railroad into Des Moines, a city to which he had moved from Illinois in 1864. An evangelist at heart, he frequently remarked during Sunday sermons, "I hammer iron all week and hammer the Gospel into peoples' hearts on Sunday."[7] He often spent evenings in evangelism also. The Faucetts and Phillips were proud of the marriage of their children, which united their families forever in their Iowa setting.

Lewis Franklin Phillips remained in Stones County until 1872. Then the frontier beckoned to him, just as it had to his father. Lewis and his wife "braved the dangers" and moved with two small daughters to Greeley County, Nebraska, to the North Loup Valley which was purported to be "one of the most beautiful valleys in the world." A son, Frank, was born in that beautiful valley, which was made even more attractive by a red cedar log cabin and the deft hand of the loving wife who graced

L.F. and Lucinda Phillips, parents of L.E. Phillips (LEP Collection).

it.[8] L. F. was well liked by the residents of the county, who elected him the first judge for the area.

Appealing though it was, the setting left much to be desired. The popular L. F. soon found the "extreme frontier" to be difficult for his young family. The constant threat of Indian attack, their long distance from trading centers, and numbing winter blizzards that destroyed his cattle were enough to urge them to leave. Then in 1874 the region was visited by a horde of grasshoppers, which totally destroyed all crops in central Nebraska, whereupon L. F. made the decision to return to Iowa. He bade his friends farewell, and finally settled near Conway in November 1874. Less than two years later, on August 18, 1876, Lucinda Josephine Phillips gave birth to a second son, Lee Eldas. Other children born to the couple included four daughters: Etta, who died at age seven; Jennie, who married R. W. Coan of Des Moines; Nellie, who married Ray Walker of Grant, Iowa; and Laura, who married J. D. Hill of Kansas City,

Missouri. There also were four other sons: Ed, Fred, and twins, Waite and Wiate, the latter dying at age 19 from a combination of a ruptured appendix and pneumonia. All three of the surviving brothers became oilmen, along with Frank and L. E.[10]

In later years, Lee Eldas spoke lovingly of his parents. His mother was beautiful both physically and spiritually. She loved her family and made it the center of her life. She seldom complained, almost never was ill, and was the last to retire after a long day. His father was universally loved and was described as a sober, industrious, scrupulously honorable man, "his word being always as good as his note."[11] He labored as a carpenter in addition to working his small 40-acre farm about two miles west of Conway. Because of a picture taken in 1900, which the family cherished, he came to be called "the man with a hoe."

L. E.'s earliest recollections were about his happy life on his father's farm. He hunted ground squirrels, robbed bird nests, and caught "crawfish in more good places than existed anywhere." He swam in a nearby creek at a big bend where the water was deepest, and once had a shirt chewed up by calves while he took a clothesless dip. He husked corn (and became state champion in that activity in 1890), dried hazel nuts, and dug potatoes for ten cents a day for A. E. Lake, a neighboring farmer, to make his spending money.

With youthful abandon and a trusted jackknife, he carved a huge "E" in the trunk of a large tree located on the homesite. And with friends he coasted on homemade sleds down nearby Swemeley Hill, as well as down the hill on Old South Street in the center of Conway. Once while playing with brother Frank on the southwest corner of their homestead, he watched as Frank accidently set some dry grass afire, which spread rapidly and came close to burning the farm house down before the fire was extinguished. Frank was strapped harshly

Phillips family portrait in 1897. Seated in front on grass, L to R, Fred, Jennie; seated on porch, L to R, Waite, Wiate, Ed, L.E., Frank, Mrs. Frank holding John, Nell; back row, L to R, L.F., Laura, Mrs. L.F.

"The Man With the Hoe," Lewis Franklin Phillips, L.E.'s father, in a photo cherished by his family.

by his father and forbidden ever to carry matches again, an edict he actually obeyed until father L. F. relented a few years before his death.

Some of the best times, L. E. recalled several years later, were those when the family visited doting grandparents on Sundays. On one occasion, in what he called "the first real tragedy of my life," a trip to Grandfather Phillips' farm had to be aborted because a balky horse refused to move. They had gotten only about 300 yards down the road when the animal halted, and the disappointment at having to stay home was great.

Another childhood memory involved the visit of several boy friends—Guy Liggett, Frank Copple, Walter Lake, and Gent Holland—to the Phillips' farm. To entertain themselves they hunted up several eggs which they broke in a partially-filled water trough. After adding lots of dirt, they produced a "wonderfully gaumy

House in Conway, Iowa, where L.E. Phillips was born, photo taken in October, 1937.

mass" about the consistency of dough. They then rolled the mass into balls and threw them against a newly painted barn. Young Lee Eldas paid for all their fun when father L. F. arrived at home that night.

As enjoyable as it was to grow up in rural Conway, it was always necessary to carry a share of the workload on the family farm. One story Lee recalled involved early farm routine. The family kept several cows and always made a lot of butter from the milk that was obtained. The brothers had to do the churning, each taking his turn to twist the crank 100 times. When the butter did not come quickly, they would take the tea kettle and pour hot water on the churn. Then, when the butter did come in, it would be white and mushy—and mother Lucinda would know what they had done. They were seldom spanked for this behavior, but everytime the boys saw a churn crank in the years that followed, they unconsciously looked for a tea kettle—and laughingly recalled the few times their mother punished them for it.[12]

When Lee was ten years old, his father sold the old

Second farm house, north of Conway, where L.E. Phillips grew up. Photo taken about 1895.

farm, borrowed $800 from a Creston, Iowa, investment company, and purchased another tract three and a half miles north of Conway. The purchase proved the "bane of my family's existence." The note was very difficult to repay, and L. F. was obliged to borrow money at usury rates just to meet the interest on it. This meant additional hardships on the family, and all had to endure periods of self denial. It is a testimonial to them that they "made a go of it."

To help out, L. E. and his brothers worked not only at home but also at odd jobs in the area. From the time he was 14, L. E. bought his clothes and earned what little spending money he had by working for neighbors after his work at home was done. He once earned "the princely sum of fifty cents per day and board" while working as a carpenter's helper for his father. So meager was his existence, he recalled that it was beyond his comprehension when he learned that some people had accumulated as much as $5000 or that they received a

L.E Phillips with Mary Lake, his second teacher at Marshall Center School. Photo taken in 1937.

wage of $100 per month. He wondered, in his youthful ascetic philosophy, why people would continue to work after they had secured savings beyond their daily needs. Later in his mature years, though the thought remained vivid in his memory, he realized that work had rewards over and above whatever financial returns it returned. Perhaps the Puritan work ethic, which he had been so carefully taught by his faithful parents, was resurfacing in his own thought processes.

While he worked, he also attended school during the winter months. There were few public schools. In 1881 he first attended Swemeley Academy, about a mile south of the farm. His first teacher was Miss Ella Wintermute. He was to visit her again in 1937 on a nostalgic trip to the place of his heritage. She was 85 at the time of that trip. He also visited Mary Lake, then 78, who was his second teacher at Marshall Center School. Little is known about his activities at those schools, but the fact that he sought these teachers out in later years and wanted to be photographed with them speaks directly to the affection he must have felt for both.[13]

In the winter of 1891, L. E. transferred to a school in nearby Sharps, walking three and one-half miles each day in the often brisk Iowa weather to be taught by Hiram Jaqua. Of his experiences there, he was less than complimentary. "The time spent in that school must have been a total loss," he wrote in his autobiographical notes, "as I do not remember distinctly having learned anything except how to smoke cigarettes." Guy Liggett taught him "the delicate art" of inhaling. The habit thus developed proved an albatross in later years, for L. E. had high blood pressure and his near chainsmoking dependence on cigarettes was harmful to his health. Though strong willed in most every other facet of his life and personal habits, he was never able to "kick the habit" although advised to do so by his physicians.

Another shift in schools occurred in 1893 when he entered "the school in Conway." At Sharps a controversy involving the teacher and some students resulted in "breaking up the entire school," and a select school was quickly organized to complete the year. L. E. did not record the facts of the controversy or of his involvement in it. One thing of value resulted from it, however; he became fast friends with Ottway Zingg, Gent Holland, and Archie Huston who "patronizingly accepted [him] into the society of Conway."

It was Ott Zingg who encouraged him to seek a higher education. In June of 1894, he followed Zingg and others to Western Normal College in Shenandoah, Iowa, for training in bookkeeping and penmanship. He was overwhelmed. He had little money and little encouragement from his parents. To earn his way, he waited on tables for his board and did janitorial work for his tuition. He recalled that he "must have been one of the greenest, most unsophisticated country boys ever

L.E. standing in front of the old Conway railroad station, still in use in 1931.

unhitched from a plow." He saw his first electric light and first modern toilet. The latter contraption, truly an oddity to him, was regulated by a lanyard, or chain, suspended from an elevated water chamber. The urge to pull it—not knowing what would happen—overpowered him, and he gave it a vigorous tug. The down rushing water seemed like Niagra Falls to him and, fearing he had broken it, he fled in fear of being found out, not knowing the facility was only operating normally.

Several important things occurred during his studies at the Shenandoah Commercial Institute and School of Penmanship of Western Normal College. His work, although he frequently was tired and even once cut his finger badly while slicing bread during his service in the kitchen, was sufficient to sustain him for most of his study period. Once he was compelled to borrow $20

from a bank in Conway to complete a term. Also, he
earned the respect and high regard of the president and
proprietor of the college, as well as the principal of the
Institute and director of his program of studies. Both
were to write glowing recommendations for him when
he graduated.[14] More important were the personal contacts and solid friendships he made during classroom
studies and extracurricular activities.

He roomed with Gent Holland in a nearby private
home. Like most college boys of any year, he lived on
the verge of uncleanliness. He had but two shirts and
was compelled at times even to share his meager ward-
robe with Gent. Their beds went unmade (and probably
without a change of sheets) for the entire term. They
worked and played hard, but it is doubtful that L. E.
absorbed much of the "learning" during his first term.
Besides, he had fallen desperately in love, but he
"couldn't make up his mind whether it would be Jose-
belle Lauder, Fanny Sterling Phillips, Jessie Nelson, or
Nora Carr." Girls had entered his life, and the pretty
and musically talented Nora Carr was forging her way,
without him realizing it fully, into his future.

During the summer of 1895, L. E. fell victim to a
mumps epidemic which took several weeks to overcome.
At the Normal School in Bedford, however, he was able
to complete the scholastic requirements for becoming
a teacher, although he still lacked the formal certification
he would obtain later. Thereafter, he worked at odd
jobs, earning approximately ten to 15 dollars per week,
which was enough to support him in a fairly active social
life in Conway during the winter months. Because he
and his friends were fun loving almost to a fault, many
townspeople, as well as their parents, felt they "were on
the road to ruination." They played "crokinole and tid-
dle winks," rode bobsleds at high speeds, and held "dev-
ilish" parties devoted to charades.

It appeared that the young people were having a last

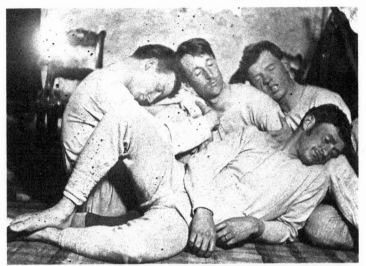

The four original members of the Never Sweat Club showing L.E. Phillips in back, center.

fling, as if hanging on to their fading boyhood's carefree existence. They were growing up, and there was the increasing, uneasy awareness of ultimate separation. Sensing it, several of them reorganized an earlier fraternal organization, founded in 1890 as the Never Sweat Club, renaming it the Anchor Club during the winter of 1895. The Never Sweat designation referred to a pledge each made never to work again as dirt farmers after they left home. The membership was composed of Archie Huston, Gent Holland, Guy Liggett, Elton Ellis, Ottway Zingg, and Lee Eldas. Later Claude Fisher and Walter Lake would round out the original membership.[15]

The Anchor Club in time would prove one of the most lasting influences in the lives of the participants. They would meet annually to "recharge their batteries" and relive the stories of their youth, and they would form an investment company which would unite them in a modest business venture.[16] The ties were cemented forever; they all remained "best friends" throughout their lives.

Such were the formative years of Lee Eldas Phillips. His life began in austerity, although he only later would realize it because all his acquaintances were no better off than he was. He progressed from a simple, unsophisticated country boy to a reasonable level of maturity through hard work and education. And he built his life around both the love of his parents and family, as well as the respect and loyalty of his friends. His was a solid foundation.

2

CAREER BEGINNINGS

The work experiences of farm life and the personal teachings of his family made indelible impressions on Lee Eldas Phillips. Being close to his family was important to him, and he seemed reluctant to leave them after his college preparation was completed. However, he spent a part of 1896 in travel with some of his friends. L. E., Guy Liggett and Gent Holland, all original members of the Never Sweat (Anchor) Club, organized an overland expedition and became small businessmen of a sort, driving a horse-drawn wagon through Iowa and Nebraska, selling furniture polish to rural families for whatever they could get in cash or farm produce, and visiting fairs. They made very little money, but during the trip L. E. claims that he got "more real education and enlightenment" than from all his previous experiences. Following that "tour," he returned to familiar surroundings to begin his early professional work.[1]

Although he had prepared for the teaching profession, he still lacked formal teacher certification, and in August of 1897 he entered the Taylor County Teachers Institute, from which he received the necessary certificate. Thus prepared, he received the first of three appointments during that school year. His first assignment was at Lock Campbell schoolhouse northeast of Conway, for which he received $22 per month for the fall term. He then accepted an assignment at Holt Township near Bedford for the winter term, and returned to the home school north of Conway for the spring term.[2] For most

Holt Township School, where L.E. Phillips taught. Picture taken in 1907.

of the year, he was able to live at home and commute each day, riding an old crippled pony which he borrowed from his father. Saving room and board expenses greatly added to his spendable income, and he was able to retire all of his outstanding debts by year's end.[3]

He enjoyed his experiences and received high commendation from Mr. Lock Campbell, the director of the first school at which he taught. When school was out, he even returned to Shenandoah to complete a course which he thought would strengthen his teaching skills.[4] During his absence from Conway, he unfortunately lost his place in fall assignments although he had been promised one for both the fall and winter terms. Not wishing to leave the area, he resumed work on his father's farm while searching for an appointment in nearby Bedford.

Almost by happenstance, a school vacancy occurred at Athelston in a district called "The Harry Nation." The last two teachers had resigned after having been thrown bodily through a window in the school house. Frank Crossin at Bedford, who located the position for him, warned L. E. that it was a tough assignment. But the young school teacher's finances were so bad by the winter term that he "was willing to go after a grizzly bear," and he persuaded the directors of the school to give him a try. His contract was made for four months at $40 per month, but the directors did not expect L. E. to last long, one stating, "The boys are twice as big as you are and they will eat you up the first day."

Lee Eldas Phillips counted 96 students that first day. A more motley group he had never encountered.[5] They were members of the vast unwashed families of the region whose home regimen consisted only of sleeping and eating and very little discipline. Baths were anathema, and clothes were practically sewn on the children, not to be taken off until spring. L. E. remembers that the odors which filled the room defied description, but hardly could be characterized as lavender or violet. Despite the stench and grime, teacher and students got along well together, so much so that the directors extended his contract for the spring term.

The *Conway Journal* on June 24, 1898, recorded an appraisal of Lee Eldas' efforts. In the news article, he was adjudged a genial, bright young gentleman whose students had greatly benefited from his teaching. The Athelston community hated to lose him, but all felt that he would inevitably "shake the dust" from his feet and return home. He had given them "entire satisfaction," the writer concluding, "Here's luck to you boy, with the wish expressed that your lines may be cast in pleasant surroundings."[6]

One of the peripheral ways that Phillips had aided his students resulted from an extracurricular activity he introduced. The United States was at war with Spain, and the students were eager to learn military drills. During morning and afternoon recesses, even after school at times, L. E. taught them such as he knew, and the students responded surprisingly well to the discipline.

L. E. himself was swept up by the patriotic fervor of the time. He was chafing to join with other Taylor and Bedford County volunteers, who then were assembling at Camp McKinley near Des Moines.

As soon as his school term was over in June, he went to the Camp, where he was told that the group was soon to go overseas, and he sought to enlist. He was dissuaded by a physician who felt his health was not good enough. Although he always would regret that he did not go with the group, he accepted the dictum. At least one Anchor Club member, Archie Huston, was in the contingent and was obliged to miss the annual meeting of the Club that year because he was serving in the Philippines.

It was back to teaching for the fall and winter terms of 1898 for L. E., this time at Marshall Township. He got on well, and patrons again praised his work. "Mr. Phillips," one account read, "is becoming one of our best young teachers and with his push and energy he is bound to succeed in his chosen profession." Another stated that he is "one of the best in the county."[7]

High praise, indeed! However, teaching at five schools in two years created apprehension in L. E.'s mind. Lack of permanency was not offset by the convenience of living at home. One by one his friends were leaving the Conway area, and despite his increasing proficiency in his profession, he felt unfulfilled and poorly remunerated. Thus he began to consider other alternatives.

Soon he was in Creston, Iowa, visiting Claude Fisher, who was in the insurance business. After lengthy discussions, L. E. decided to become Fisher's associate and returned home to discuss the change with his parents. He faced unexpected and severe opposition. To them $40 per month and a promise of permanent appointment at Marshall Township was the opportunity of a lifetime. They urged him not to give up the teaching profession. Somehow he convinced them of the wisdom of his decision, and he moved to Creston at the close of the winter school term. The Creston newspaper printed an announcement of his arrival on March 27, 1899. He moved into the office of Claude Fisher in a building on North Maple Street, and although theirs was not a partnership they aided each other in developing their businesses. Through Elton Ellis, his cousin, who was then in business in Des Moines, he added to his list of insurance company affiliates. One of them was the Greenwich Insurance Company of New York City, a firm first organized in 1834. L. E. became the local agent for the company, working with Ed Bowden, who was a special supervisory agent for the parent company.[8]

L. E.'s older brother, Frank, already resided in Creston and by 1897 had become the successful owner-operator of a group of tonsorial parlors. L. E. was invited to move in with Frank and his wife, which he did for a short time. But city life was "no pot at the end of the rainbow," and insurance did not sell itself. L. E. at first sold little of his product, and only his pride diverted his attention from his hunger pains. Finally he found the magic combination. His marketing techniques improved and his sales increased to a level which returned him greater income than his school teaching had afforded.

One of his contacts during that period was George B. Rex. Rex and his son owned a lumber and coal company in Creston, which was quite successful. L. E. must have impressed the elder Rex, for in May of 1899, he extended an offer to Phillips to join the firm. The offer was exactly what L. E. had always wanted. He would travel as a salesman and receive a monthly salary plus expenses. For some strange reason, which he silently confessed later was foolhardy, Phillips turned the job down, saying that his business was so good he could not give it up. Rex must have sensed that L. E. would change his mind, for the offer later was renewed and accepted.

L.E. Phillips with George B. Rex for whom he worked as a traveling salesman. Photo taken in 1937.

Phillips started to work for George Rex and Son on July 2, 1899, at a salary of $50 per month and expenses.[9]

Lee Eldas Phillips was delighted with the new arrangement. He sold his insurance agency to Tom Davis for $100 and took to the road with George Rex, who had consented to make one trip to help acquaint him with his business contacts. Interestingly, L. E. had trouble keeping his expense accounts balanced, despite the fact that he was a graduate of a business school. Because of his ineptness, he lost most of his first month's salary and all the money he had accumulated after only one month on the road. With Rex's help, this did not happen again.

George Rex valued his new employee and was impressed with his wisdom and vigor. Not only did he raise L. E.'s salary to $65 per month for August and September, but then increased it to $75 per month for November through December. Moreover, he sanctioned a plan which allowed his traveling salesman to spend most of his time on the road with expenses paid, thus permitting L. E. to avoid paying room and board.

On January 2, 1900, L. E. seemed to be sitting on top of the world. After a briefing session that day with George Rex on his year's assignment, he learned that his salary was being increased to $1000 per year. He was given a bigger territory with some of the larger towns like Omaha to call on. Rex urged him to leave the next day, and, with his typical enthusiasm, L. E. charged out across the lumberyard.

There he met a familiar fixture in the yard, a faithful old man known as "Dad." He was a general handyman whose tasks included sawing wood. L. E. was unusually distressed by what he saw: a 75 year old man, feet wrapped in gunny sacks tied with rope, body protected by a tattered overcoat, hands covered with pitiable mittens, and head shielded by an old cap. By contrast, Phillips was the essence of success: new suit, raised salary, broader responsibility, and vigorous youth. Stunned by the anomaly, L. E. asked "Dad" how much wood he could saw each day and how much he was paid per cord. "If I work right hard," the old man responded, "I can saw one cord and get seventy-five cents for doing it." The impression left by this encounter was profound. L. E. resolved "right then and there" that he literally would not be so victimized or destitute when he reached the age of 75.[10]

Success followed success in his traveling sales position for the company, which by 1902 had become known as the Rex Coal and Mining Company of Creston, Iowa. Salary increases and a larger territory, which by July of that year embraced the several states served by the Burlington and Rock Island Railroad, clearly evidenced his growing importance to George B. Rex. Accordingly, Rex then offered L. E. an opportunity to become one of the original incorporators of a new venture in Knoxville, Iowa.

The new venture, The Hawkeye Mining Company, which first was organized in October, was formally incorporated on November 13, 1902. That same day also marked another milestone in Lee Eldas' life: The *Creston Daily Examiner* carried the announcement of his impending marriage on November 26, 1902, to Lenora Carr, daughter of Mr. and Mrs. James A. Carr of Bedford, Iowa. She was described as "beautiful, lovely, and accomplished," he as "one of Creston's brightest young men." Undoubtedly the two developments were directly related.[11] George Rex wanted L. E. to move to Knoxville to organize and manage the new company, and the young couple must have decided to start their life together at the new location.

Lenora Carr was, indeed, a lovely and talented young lady. At the time of her wedding she was a striking beauty with a cultured, stately poise. Her Bedford parents were industrious and religious, and had sought to provide the best training for their children. Lenora followed the study of music and became an accomplished teacher of piano and organ. She had attended schools in Conway and Bedford, pursued her studies in Shenandoah at Western Normal College, and later studied at Drake University in Des Moines.[12]

Node, as she was called (pronounced Nodie), was extremely well liked, and a number of young suitors always expressed romantic interest in her. She once served as postmistress for Conway and taught private music lessons in the family home. Her students performed well, both in informal sessions and at recitals, especially at the Conway Opera House where admission frequently was charged.[13] As standard format, Miss Carr always opened a recital with a favorite rendition and closed it with another. Because of the scarcity of enter-

L.E. and Lenora shown in 1896 at Lover's Retreat near Conway, Iowa.

tainment in rural Iowa towns, such recitals were regarded as top experiences and were well attended.[14]

Node and L. E. were well acquainted with each other and frequently socialized at gatherings in the vicinity of Conway and Bedford. Hayrides, picnics, and evening charade parties often cast them together. A romance began to bud as early as 1896, when photographs of them in partial embrace were lodged in the family album. One picture, depicting Nora's home in Bedford, shows a porch and swing "where Node and I used to watch the moon." They also were shown at a site referred to as "Old Lover's Retreat," a small arbor near a damsite in a quiet part of Conway.[15]

Perhaps a strong reason why L. E. was reluctant to leave Conway after his graduation from college was to avoid the pain of being away from Node. And the lonely life of a traveling salesman must certainly have quickened his desire to hasten the day when he could claim her as his bride. Still, there was a career to be fashioned and a stable, dependable income to be achieved. Six years of waiting must have seemed interminable, but it finally ended with their marriage at the home of her parents in Bedford, at 5:30 p.m. on Wednesday, November 26, 1902. Officiating was Elder Lee Ferguson of the Christian Church, the church of the Carr family where Node also served regularly as organist. Miss Eva Carr, sister of the bride, was maid of honor; Gent Holland, L. E.'s boyhood chum, was best man.[16]

News references to the wedding were numerous both before and after it took place. At least four members of the Anchor Club attended: Guy Liggett of Omaha, Elton Ellis and Gent Holland of Des Moines, and Claude Fisher of Creston. Also attending from Creston were Frank Phillips and his wife, and George B. Rex. It was an important social occasion for Bedford and vicinity. L. E. and Lenora were popular and promising young people, postnuptial comments indicated. The *Creston Morning American* praised Node as possessing "all the graces and accomplishments which qualify one for society, and which qualifies a woman to be queen of the home circle." Of Phillips it was said that he was "an enterprising man of business, well qualified for the duties of life which lie before him." Mention was made of his position with Rex Coal and Mining Company, and also of the fact that a new venture would be opened in Knoxville. "Mr. Phillips will be manager, and the newly married people will make their home in Knoxville."[17]

Thus the combined venture had begun. The Phillips arrived in Knoxville on December 5, 1902, and took up residence in Parson's House, a room and board hotel which cost them $12 per week. They remained as tenants until May of 1903 when they moved to the Josie Mikinzie house. The move was imperative; their first child was

The Phillips' first house in Knoxville, Iowa, where they lived from March, 1903, to June, 1905. Both Philip Rex and L.E., Jr., were born in this house.

well on the way and would eventually arrive on October 3, 1903. The baby was lovely, and the young couple were delighted. Only a few days passed before a first picture was taken of Philip Rex Phillips by his doting parents.[18]

Meanwhile, the Hawkeye Mining Company had begun operations. The incorporators were Frank D. Ball, George B. Rex, Lee Eldas Phillips, I. O. James, and Fred J. Spies. Capital stock for the company was set at $15,000 divided into 150 shares of $100 each. The object, as stated in the Articles of Incorporation, was to mine and sell coal. By October 1902, when the company was first organized, L. E. had accumulated $1500 which he invested in the company. He at first was enthusiastic about his new undertaking. At the initial meeting of the directors and stockholders of the corporation, L. E. was elected secretary and general manager. George Rex was elected president.[19]

*Early photo of Philip
Rex, going for a daily
ride in July, 1904.*

Essentially, it was a local company, and its early success was a source of satisfaction to the investors. Corporate properties, mostly lease rights, were located in
Marion County near Knoxville.[20] It was hailed as a
source of potential prosperity for the city. Then troubles
began. L. E. was later to characterize the development
as "about the most unwise and unsound business venture
we could have made." The coal found on their leases
was of poor quality, and the mines proved difficult to
work. A severe shortage of capital limited change and
equipment purchases, and L. E. felt himself to be too
inexperienced to provide effective leadership during the
growing crisis. Only a coal strike in the East postponed
the severity of their problems during the first year's
operation. Coal of almost any quality was in demand
during that period.

But ill winds were forecast for the Hawkeye Mining
Company by the newspapers in the area. Even the com-
ings and goings of L. E., as reported in local newspapers,

testified that he was serving more in the capacity of a salesman than as the general manager of the mine. Financial disaster struck in 1903 when a strike began at the Hawkeye properties. Because of recent experiences, it had been predicted. Phillips and P. M. Myers, who represented the local Mine Workers Union, had only recently attended a state convention of Mine Operators and Mine Workers in Des Moines. There they learned that the national meeting of the Coal Miners and Mine Workers Union for ten days had debated an owners' proposal to cut miners' wages in the United States by 5-1/4%.[21] Friction resulted in tensions, and serious trouble appeared imminent. It came at Hawkeye not only in the form of a strike but also in destructive violence. The mines were flooded, production halted, and the stockpile of inferior coal became unsalable. There was no capital reserve and no cash flow; the company finally closed the mine early in 1904.

The loss was difficult to take. Not only had a $1500 investment evaporated in less than two years, but also a much needed monthly income was gone. With a second child on the way, L. E. felt the pressures of a man of affairs without means, and he began to search for a new job. He did not meet with early success. Liquidation of Hawkeye properties was begun, but it would take until April of 1905 to dispose of the assets. Even then, L. E.'s share of the net proceeds was a mere $80. What had begun as a grand venture had resulted in virtual bankruptcy for him.

As fate would have it, his despair soon was mitigated by his brother Frank. For some time there had been serious stirrings in the Indian Territory, and rumors abounded about the "monstrous possibilities" in oil exploration. Frank heard of the possibilities from an old preacher friend of his, C. B. Larrabee, who had served for a time near Bartlesville as a Methodist missionary to the Indians. The two men had met at the St. Louis Ex-

Bartlesville, Indian Territory, in 1903, as L.E. and Frank Phillips saw it during their exploratory trips. (LEP Collection.)

position and the clergyman had made his description so believable that Frank was persuaded to make an exploratory trip there himself. And later in 1903 Frank and his father-in-law, John Gibson, made two trips to Bartlesville to check out the possibilities. Frank had just returned from one of those trips when he called to ask L. E. to meet him in Des Moines at the Kirkwood Hotel. Frank was beaming with excitement about "a new scheme" and wanted to discuss a joint venture with his younger brother.[22]

The meeting in Des Moines was destined to reshape the lives of the entire Phillips family. Frank's enthusiasm was not matched by L. E. when he first heard about the developments near Bartlesville. Exploration for oil sounded all too much like his most recent experiences in attempting the mining of coal. The memory of that failure was still too vivid to kindle reciprocal enthusiasm in the younger Phillips. Besides, the Indian Territory was undeveloped and not a fit place for raising a young family. Moreover, Lee Eldas was broke, and there was a more urgent need to earn his sustenance than to begin a new venture in a "foreign country." Additionally, he had a deep-seated belief that by some divine right, all oil in America belonged to the Standard Oil Company which would frown at any intrusion on its domain.

All arguments to the contrary, a penniless L. E. succumbed to the need for making money, and his resistance evaporated. He agreed to join Frank in the new undertaking, and they set out quickly to develop a financial package to fund their operations. L. E. also agreed to accompany his older brother to Bartlesville in order to gain first-hand knowledge of the possibilities. His first exploratory trip was made in mid-1904, and the Conway and Creston newspapers, ever alert for a news item, reported L. E.'s departure and his return.[23] From the date of that trip, L. E. and Frank became almost inseparable partners. Because of their ability to work together, theirs was an enviable professional relationship. From the leases they obtained on that trip, they were to set in motion what one day would become the Phillips Petroleum Company. Though much remained to be accomplished before oil exploration could begin, it is obvious that both brothers were highly satisfied with what they saw in the Indian Territory. Nothing could dissuade them from making the grand attempt to become oilmen.

They were to return again in late February of 1905 for what was L. E.'s second trip. This time he remained several weeks, during which he and Frank opened an office, secured a driller, and started their first well. The Phillips Petroleum Company had begun, but the energetic young brothers were too busy to think much about the future. Indeed, L. E. was still too leery about his most recent financial setback in coal mining to relax very much. He worked long hours, slept few, and worried about the infant son and pregnant young wife whom he had left behind at their Knoxville home.

But the stage was set and the countdown had begun. Only a few months separated the Phillips brothers from their first gusher, which would blow briefly into the atmosphere and subsequently be harnessed to flow steadily into their reservoirs.

3

THE BANKER
1905-1919

Oil exploration in Oklahoma was but a few years old when the Phillips brothers arrived in Bartlesville. The town had few conveniences. The landscape was covered with derricks, strewn with drilling equipment and accessories, and dotted by crude out-buildings which served every function imaginable. There was but one two-story brick building which seemed sturdy enough but out of character for its setting. There were no paved streets, few trees, still fewer sidewalks, and plenty of mud when it rained. Still, it was an honest town, dedicated almost to a single cause—exploration for oil.[1]

Despite the flurry of activity, some of the rampant enthusiasm about drilling for oil seemed out of phase with reality. There was only a modest market for crude oil, as evidenced by its low price of "thirty to thirty-six" cents per barrel. The great age of gasoline consumption lay in the future. Kerosene and grease were the principal products, and their main uses were for lighting, heating, cooking, and for greasing farm implements. Some farmers also used oil derivatives to smear on livestock to protect them from lice and ticks. Such uses seem ignoble for a resource which has now become so essential for industrial production and creature comfort.[2]

To go to Bartlesville with a chance for success required planning. Soon after their meeting at the Kirkwood Hotel in Des Moines early in 1904, L. E. and Frank developed a strategy: "We were to furnish the ideas and

*In early Bartlesville, streams had to be forded since there were
no bridges spanning them.*

the enthusiasm and someone else was to furnish the
money." They turned to John Gibson, Frank's banker
father-in-law, who helped them form the Anchor Oil
and Gas Company. Several of Gibson's business associates, among them F. D. Ball and Stewart Spaulding of
Creston, Ben Martin of Salem, Illinois, and H. K. Bur-
kett of Omaha, Nebraska, helped organize the Company
with an authorized capital of $100,000 and paid-in cap-
ital of $15,000. It also seems certain that some part of
a $20,000 wedding gift which John Gibson gave to Frank
and Jane Gibson Phillips upon their marriage, plus an
equal amount of prior savings, became a part of this
capital formation.[3]

Integral to the Anchor development was an agreement which called for L. E. and Frank to sell additional
shares of stock on commission in order to increase the
operational reserves. For L. E. it was a godsend; he was
broke, and the commissions he received provided sustenance for his family. He also took some of his commissions in Anchor stock. Between trips to the Bartlesville
area, both faithfully fulfilled their agreement, and by

February of 1905 all signs were positive enough for the brothers to embark on their new adventure in oil.

In late February, they secured an office and started a well which was named Holland No. 1. L. E. became office manager, putting to good use his commercial education and the business experience he had gained while working for George B. Rex. Frank moved his family to Bartlesville in the spring of 1905, living at the Almeda Hotel, but because Node was expecting a second child, L. E. delayed moving his family, opting instead to commute to his Knoxville, Iowa, home as often as he could. He was there on June 23, 1905, when Holland No. 1 blew in and was delighted when he received a telegram from Frank saying that it had been completed.

The unbounded enthusiasm which L. E. felt was soon bulnted by the fact that Holland No. 1 was in what is now termed a "pocket of oil" and quickly ceased production. Disappointed but not discouraged, L. E. awaited the arrival on June 3, 1905, of his second son, Lee Eldas Phillips, Jr., closed his Knoxville home soon thereafter, and lodged his wife temporarily with her parents in Bedford, partly out of the need for security for his young sons and partly out of economic necessity. L. E. still had a personal cash flow problem which was made all the more dismal by lack of drilling success, which also was proving costly. Although he returned to the Indian Territory immediately, he would wait until September before moving his family to Bartlesville.[4]

Not only was Holland No. 1 a non-producer, but also the Phillips' second and third wells were entirely dry. "It began to look," L. E. recorded in his autobiographical notes, "as though there was no place in the oil business for anyone except the Standard Oil." But opportunities still abounded, and there were enough reported successes to spur the brothers on. Despite the fact that L. E. was often heard to remark in later years that "if we hadn't hit the Anna Anderson, we'd have been back on the farm in Iowa," it is highly unlikely that the Phillips brothers would have accepted defeat so readily.[5]

It was the age of "boom and bust." Some men struck it big one month and lost their earnings in dry holes the next. As L. E. had written to his friend in Knoxville, a few dry holes were essential to the appreciation of a good well. With three non-producers for experience, L. E. and Frank were due some appreciation. They had had quite enough "bust"; it was now time to balance the scale with a little "boom." It came on September 6, 1905. At a well site named Anna Anderson No. 1, fortune of a type which makes sacrifice seem imminently worthwhile boomed for L. E. and Frank Phillips. The well made 250 barrels a day. It was magnificent. In retrospect the event seemed less a crisis than it was, for success tends to blot out the anxieties engendered by repeated failures. The facts are irrefutable, however: there was, indeed, but sufficient money to drill a fourth and final well. And the Anchor Oil and Gas investment capital was virtually depleted; few if any new stockholders could have been recruited because of the impact of the previous dry holes. Worse, the selection of the Anna Anderson site was made more for convenience of location than from any sophisticated geological report. Sheer luck dominated their efforts.[6] Would it have been "back to the farm in Iowa" had the well proven dry?

Unquestionably not. The Phillips brothers were men of destiny; theirs was a feeling that the future held something special in store for them. Nowhere is it more in evidence than in the way both revered and recorded their heritage, as if paving the roads they traveled with cobblestones indelibly marked for the convenience of those who one day would measure their paths to greatness. Greatness began on September 6, 1905. Anna Anderson No. 1 proved the first of a consecutive string of more than 80 successful wells before the Phillips brothers again would drill a non-producer.

The five Phillips brothers, L to R, Ed, Waite, Fred, Frank, and L.E., in Bartlesville about 1907. All five became oilmen.

The well was named for an eight-year-old Delaware Indian girl on whose land allotment the drilling took place. She had been living with her maternal grandparents near Dewey, Indian Territory, when she received an individual allotment of tribal lands, a transaction sanctioned by Congress in 1902. Her parcel was only 80 acres and was located at the juncture of the Big and Little Caney rivers. Just how the Phillips obtained the lease rights is not known, but the results of it are now history. Anna Anderson ultimately became "the richest little Indian girl in Oklahoma."[7] L. E. and Frank Phillips did not fare badly themselves.

Success breeds success, especially in a bust-or-boom environment. Not only were more wells brought in, but the Anchor Oil and Gas Company also prospered. Soon there were more than 100 stockholders and an additional $100,000 was realized from stock sales. Having satisfied the Anchor shareholders with the potential returns on investments from the Anna Anderson lease, the two older brothers, along with younger brother

Anna Anderson #1 in September, 1907, the first successful oil well drilled by the Phillips brothers.

Waite, then formed a new operation which they named the Lewcinda Oil Company, in honor of their parents Lewis and Lucinda. Waite, as it turned out, remained only a short time with Lewcinda, preferring instead to be independent in his business arrangements. He sold his interests in Lewcinda to L. E. and Frank. Waite would soon enjoy fabulous success in Tulsa and Los Angeles in oil, banking and real estate development.[8]

It was then that another cobblestone was implanted. L. E. records that in July of 1905 a long-time resident

L.E. Phillips, Philip Rex Phillips (his son) and Frank Phillips at the Anna Anderson well site.

of Bartlesville encouraged him and Frank seriously to consider the "great opportunity in the banking and trust company business." They attempted something of a feasibility study by seeking the counsel of several businessmen, after which they surmised there was a need for another financial institution in Bartlesville. Moreover, the venture would afford them the opportunity to diversify their investments, thus cushioning them against some of the adverse impacts of the highs and lows of oil prospecting.

As a result, Frank and L. E. Phillips organized the Citizens Bank and Trust Company with a capital of $50,000. It later was chartered as a state bank. Frank was elected president, and L. E. was made cashier. The younger brother was "heals over head" in debt, but he managed to borrow $10,000 from the Guttenburg State

The Bartlesville National Bank (indicated by arrow) owned by the Phillips brothers.

Bank of Guttenburg, Iowa, with which he purchased ten shares of stock at a par value of $1000.[9] They officially opened for business on December 4, 1905, and the first day's customer response was encouraging. The bank proved a wise investment.

And so it happened: Anna Anderson No. 1 in September, the Citizens Bank and Trust in December. The early cobblestones were clearly labeled. By then, some of the financial pressures were diminishing, but L. E. still had little cash money and found conditions for his family to be "far from satisfactory" in Bartlesville. Prices were high, and his small four-room house lacked bath facilities until he added them at his own expense. Moreover, he had been obliged to pay a full six months' rent in advance. That, in current vernacular, left him strapped.

Because the town was growing, the bank prospered. Three competing banks already were operating in the town and were resentful of their newest constituent. A brisk rivalry developed, the Phillips brothers soon re-

Interior view, Bartlesville National Bank.

alizing that the intent was to force the Citizens Bank and
Trust out of business. But with shrewdness and good
business acumen, Citizens prospered and grew anyway.
L. E. later noted with understandable pride that of the
three competing institutions, one failed and the other
two were bought and absorbed by the principal officers
of Citizens Bank and Trust: Frank and L. E. Phillips.[10]

L. E. and Frank early made a pact that once the two
were permanently settled and reasonably adjusted to
Bartlesville, Frank would look after their oil interests
and L. E. would run the bank. For years, they held to
this stratagem. L. E. became the chief operating officer
for Citizens, personally keeping the bank books by day
and then doing those for the oil businesses at night on
a schedule which began at 7:00 a.m. and ended some-
where between 11:00 p.m. and 2:00 a.m. each day. L.

E. was, as many have described him, a workaholic. It probably is true that he derived his greatest professional satisfaction from his identity as one of the premier bankers in Midwestern America.

Frank, meanwhile, handled the oil business out of a small room at the rear of the bank. That part of their business was complicated by the fact that the Department of the Interior had established rules which precluded any company from holding more than 4800 acres of Indian land. Thus in order to expand their oil lease holdings, it became necessary, over an extended period of time, to create 15 separate corporations.[11] For L. E. this meant a new set of books for each, explaining at least in part why he spent such long hours each day in the fiscal management of the Phillips' resources.

Success on the banking front progressed steadily. On January 29, 1906, a little over a month after opening, deposits were $37,377.11. By September 23, 1908, the bank announced deposits totalling $375,728.72, and in December of that year, L. E. received his first bank dividend check in the amount of $80.[12] Not even the Panic of 1907 seemed to slow the growth, although there were months of stress during which L. E. acknowledged that his experiences hardened him and made him a better banker. The Citizens Bank and Trust Company, like most financial institutions, had to devise ways to stop customers from "making a run" on the bank. A policy of prohibiting cash withdrawals of more than $20 was adopted and for the most part proved enforceable until November of 1907 when one unidentified but notorious Oklahoma "bad man" entered the Citizens Bank and demanded all his deposits in cash. "Suffice to say," L. E. remembered, "he got the money due to two big six shooters he had on him." It has been said that there is an exception to every policy, and L. E. showed wisdom in exercising good judgment in this case.[13]

Wisdom and good judgment were characteristics of Lee Eldas Phillips which were manifested in sound management techniques as well as personal magnetism. He loved people and always sought to assist them in achieving their highest ambitions. One rancher, Heber Skinner, would long remember L. E. with deep fondness as "one of the finest men I ever saw." Phillips had loaned money to Skinner when he first came into the Indian Territory "way back in 1906 and 1907." One of Skinner's most treasured possessions was a photograph showing him, among others, with L. E. Phillips and another famous Oklahoma resident, Will Rogers. It was prominently displayed in his ranch home.[14]

The Citizens Bank emerged from the Panic months in a strong cash position, and the Phillips brothers decided to broaden their activities. They made a wise decision to bring William Johnstone from a health-enforced retirement into the Citizens Bank. Johnstone was one of the pioneers of Northern Oklahoma, and was affectionately known as "the father of the banking industry in Bartlesville." He was named Vice President and elected a director. He assumed his duties in the fall of 1908.[15]

Johnstone's appointment brought L. E. much-needed relief, although it is doubtful if either of the men was able to reduce his daily number of work hours. Almost immediately two new business ventures were announced. On August 1, 1908, it was learned that L. E. and Frank had purchased 35 acres of undeveloped land for $50,000 in Bartlesville, "probably the most valuable of any, similarly situated, in Northern Oklahoma." Known as the Johnstone Heights Addition, after its former owner, Leo Johnstone, it was bounded by Osage Avenue on the west, by Seventh Street on the north, by Shawnee Avenue on the East, and by Eleventh Street on the south. The acreage was to be laid out and subdivided into residential lots, which were described as some of the most beautiful building sites in all of Bartlesville. "This deal," the news announcement stated, "is one of the largest that has ever been pulled off in the local real estate market."[16]

By year's end "some of the best people" in the city had made their selection of a lot, and home development was soon to begin on this "high and airy property." However, some criticism of the Johnstone Heights project surfaced after the Phillips brothers and their newly acquired developer/partner, Harve Pemberton, requested that the city government pave the streets in the subdivision. Some citizens believed that the new section was receiving preferred treatment and complained loudly about it. However, when it was noted that the developers had spent "thousands of dollars" on street grading and sidewalks, much of the criticism declined. The streets eventually were paved at the Phillips brothers' expense. Despite these additional costs, the lots were advertised at a beginning price of only $600 and up. Frank built a handsome new residence in the subdivision, adding "beauty and dignity to the property."[17] L. E. later would purchase a large brick home and add significantly to it on a site just across the street from his brother's mansion. Thus the brothers Phillips became town developers in addition to their other interests.

Close on the heels of their entry into real estate, L. E. and Frank ventured still farther into banking. On November 7, 1908, they announced that they were purchasing one of their rivals, the Bartlesville National Bank, an institution which had been organized in 1902 by William Johnstone. All the stock was bought by the "active officers" of the Citizens Bank and Trust Company at "a very handsome premium" to the BNB shareholders. So attractive was the offer that it was accepted unanimously by the 18 directors/stockholders.[18] The takeover was more than fiscal. The bank actually was physically relocated overnight into the Citizens Bank building, and the two institutions, which operated separately, opened under the same roof the next banking day. Some of the BNB personnel were moved and retained, but the officers and directors were either retired or removed. They were replaced by Citizens Bank administrators; in fact, the CB&T and the BNB had the same slate of officers, starting with Frank Phillips as president and concluding with L. E. Phillips as cashier.

The move was hailed by some, criticized by others. The *Bartlesville Enterprise*, in announcing the transaction, praised the Phillips as "the active kind of financiers who are certain to keep the opposition awake nights." The *Independence Reporter* characterized them as "among the most tireless hustlers" in Oklahoma, to whom the "strenuous life is normal."[19] However, the takeover and joint operation of the banks drew protests from the state banking commissioner and the Federal Controller of Currency, but did not prevent the unusual association.[20] Indeed, the same set of officers administered both banks for more than three years, until the arrangement no longer served the best interests of the Phillips brothers.

Definite advantages accrued to the simultaneous operation of the banks. Considerable savings resulted from a single slate of officers, joint occupancy of the same building, and standardized accounting practices. Moreover, some customers preferred a state bank, such as the Citizens Bank and Trust, because it not only could make loans on real estate but also could offer modest protection of deposits by virtue of a controversial state guaranty law. Other customers preferred a national bank, such as the Bartlesville National Bank, largely because of the greater confidence engendered by an institution which was regulated and "protected" by federal law. Each type had its advantages and attractions to particular customers, and the brothers Phillips now had assembled the advantages of both under a single umbrella— with resources totalling almost a million dollars to meet their needs.

In time L. E. became an outspoken critic of the state's

controversial guaranty law, a statute which required "solvent and well managed banks to pay the losses of failed banks."[21] It was an early scheme designed to protect deposits by spreading potential losses from bank failures among all Oklahoma banks. The effect of the law caused many customers to select a state bank, which carried this indirect guarantee of their deposits, over a national bank, which was not yet protected by federal deposit insurance laws. Such a philosophy and resulting practices were alien to an Iowa farm boy turned Oklahoma banker whose Christian and Spartan upbringing had taught him hard work, honesty, and responsibility for one's personal actions and security. To him the guaranty law was demeaning to trustworthy and resolute bankers, who would be required to underwrite with hard earned assets the incompetent or dishonest banker who might mismanage his depositors' resources.

He would take his fight to the governor and to the state legislature, and in the process be roundly criticized by Charles N. Haskell, editor of the *New State Tribune*.[22] He was accused of benefiting from the public acceptance of the law (customers actually showed a definite preference for state banks because of the advantage of depositor's protection) while attacking it under a thinly veiled guise of fiscal conservatism. For all his efforts, the results were unproductive. The law remained unchanged. But L. E. was determined to avoid the potential consequences of the law.

To do so would require the consolidation of the Citizens Bank and Trust with the Bartlesville National. It was finally consummated on April 1, 1911, with an announced capital stock of $100,000, and an additional surplus of almost $50,000. There was no change in ownership, management, or policy. The officers, by then quite well-known in Bartlesville, were Frank Phillips, president; H. J. Holm, vice president; and L. E. Phillips, in his familiar role as cashier. By December 5, 1911, the

THE BANKER / 49

Bartlesville National Bank issued a condensed statement showing assets and deposits of $914,163.60. Finally, during the year 1912, the BNB, advertising itself as "a bank for all people" which paid four percent per annum on all savings accounts, passed the million dollar plateau in total resources. To serve its customers better, the bank began, in 1914, to publish the *Bartlesville National Bank News*, a monthly paper with timely advice on the value of saving and having a bank account, as well as about farm notes, oil and gas news and other matters of local interest.[23]

Another fortuitous development occurred when the Phillips brothers were able to persuade the United States Indian Agency at Muskogee to allow their bank to act as guardians for Indian deposits. This proved a very profitable addition to their banking operations.[24]

Lee Eldas' role in the consolidated bank reflected more than his title as cashier would indicate. With Frank's activities confined more and more to oil exploration, L. E. became the equivalent of a chief operating officer with the title of vice president. He now had sufficient personnel to handle the bank's general accounting and auditing requirements, although he never fully relinquished his authority over those vital functions, and he was able to spend more time in management and public relations. He excelled in both areas.

One humorous event, which sorely tested his public relations talents, occurred shortly after the consolidation. One afternoon two women entered the BNB, "one purporting to be blind and the other acting as guide." They approached L. E.'s desk and laid down a card which blind people used as an opening request for a donation. Lee stated that he contributed regularly to appropriate charitable organizations and waved them away. He was rewarded by his greeters with an epithet "not considered good form in polite society."

The two solicitors then proceeded to work the employees and customers of the bank. In his polite manner, Phillips again asked them to leave. When they declined, he opened the bank door and insisted a third time. The woman guide became infuriated, raised her umbrella, and struck L. E. across the shoulder, "letting loose a flood of billingsgate that would do credit to a longshoreman." Frightened by the quick development, the alleged blind woman suddenly opened her eyes and made a dash for the sidewalk, hotly pursued by her former guide. A fun-loving Lee Eldas Phillips quipped that in the future he would run should any of the blind again come in the bank.[25]

L. E.'s participation in state-wide banking activities marked him early as one of Oklahoma's brightest and most visible personalities. He attended his first bank meeting in Vinita in 1906, and by 1910 was elected to the executive committee of the Oklahoma Bankers Association (the OBA, as it was often called). At the 1911 annual meeting of the Association, he was asked to speak on the subject of taxation, an address that was published in the *Oklahoma Banker* in its April 1911 issue. Hailed by some as a major political and economic statement, it deplored "double taxation," resented the fact that the costs of collecting personal taxes often approximated the revenue derived, and strongly urged the bankers of Oklahoma to insist that the governor appoint a tax commission to adjust the inequities of the state's tax structure. He was, as one analyst wrote, a devotee of Henry George's single tax theory and thought it the most logical solution to the evils of the nation's tax laws. His statesmanship brought him additional recognition, and he was called upon to deliver other addresses on the same subject.[26]

The Bartlesville banker continued to move up the administrative ladder of the OBA. In 1915 he was elected vice president. The honor came without L. E. having to campaign for it, and he was so surprised that he had to decline the invitation to give an acceptance speech, something he rarely refused since he enjoyed public speaking. The following year he was elected to the top position in the Association, the first and only banker from Bartlesville to be so honored until Walter V. Allison of the First National Bank (a Phillips institution) was chosen in 1977.[27]

Bartlesville expressed pride in L. E. for having been elected president of the Association and for bringing honor to the city. "L. E. Phillips," a Bartlesville newspaper recorded, "is still on the sunny side of forty and has been for the past ten years one of the most active and untiring workers for . . . the best welfare of Bartlesville." His new honor, the article concluded, would unquestionably bring recognition to the city and advance its interests.[28]

His activities throughout the year certainly did just that. Speaking on May 13, 1916, to the Rotary Club of Bartlesville, of which he was a member, he delivered what was termed "one of the best civic talks ever made" in the city. He called on the membership to forget themselves, fight self-satisfaction, and give of their time to make a better Bartlesville. In September he was in Kansas City attending the annual convention of the American Bankers Association. He received front-page recognition complete with picture, which depicted him as "one of the live wire bankers of the Southwest." He responded to the compliment by flattering the host city: "Kansas City promises more than any other city in the West . . . .If you are quoting me . . . you can't make it too strong."[29]

As president of the OBA, he sought also to bring an outstanding American to the state when he invited former president William Howard Taft to speak to the OBA. Unfortunately, Taft could not accept the invitation because of a full calendar. He also tried unsuccessfully to bring Major Paul Malone from the Chicago Headquarters of the War Department to speak on the subject of "Military Preparedness."[30]

Fate often plays a prominent role in the lives of those destined for greatness. Because of the volatile, fluctuating nature of the oil business and because of the seeming stability and growth of their banking enterprise, the Phillips brothers decided to sell all their oil holdings sometime in 1915 and 1916 in order to concentrate on the banking business. They sold their production and most of their leases to the Tidal Oil Company, but they were unable to divest themselves of some lease rights in the Osage Lands because Department of Interior regulations forbade their reassignment. Ultimately, because of increasing war demands for petroleum and because the lure of the oil business was too great to resist, the brothers would drill on their Osage leases with such success that by 1917 they had formed the now famous Phillips Petroleum Company.[31]

L. E. for two more years would be the active banker in the family and would continue to pile up accolades for his efforts. He once was asked to move to New York as an executive of a major bank; he declined to the great relief of his family who did not wish to leave Bartlesville. But by 1919, the Phillips Petroleum Company was growing at such a pace that L. E., at Frank's insistence, retired as an active banker and joined his brother full-time in their oil operations. He continued to carry the title of vice president at the bank, but would act only in an advisory capacity to H. J. Holm, to whom he relinquished the operational responsibilities of the Bartlesville National Bank. Phillips also continued his service as a director.[32]

Shortly after this change of status, another giant step upward was taken when the Bartlesville National Bank purchased and merged assets with still another rival, the First National Bank of Bartlesville. This was "the most important financial transaction in local banking history," and brought a combined resource base of approximately $6.5 million under single management.[33] The BNB operation and personnel were moved to the more spacious building previously owned by the stockholders of the First National Bank, and the officers of the newly consolidated bank were essentially those not only of the BNB but also of the old Citizens Bank and Trust of a decade before. Listed as president was Frank Phillips and as vice president, L. E. Phillips. H. J. Holm, since 1919 the "active" vice president and chief operations officer of the BNB, was named to the same post of the revamped First National Bank hierarchy.

Lee Eldas Phillips' reputation as a banker was widely recognized. By 1921 he was listed among 43 financiers at the American Bankers Association in Los Angeles as "Bankers Who Made History." He had been active in the ABA for more than a decade and rarely missed an annual meeting. His involvement brought him early election in 1917 as vice president, and subsequently (1917-1918) a two-year term as a member of the executive committee of the ABA.[34]

He narrowly missed being appointed in 1914 to a directorship on the Federal Reserve Bank for District 10, then being established in Kansas City under the Regional Bank Act.[35] He was widely endorsed by his friends and banking associates from the Oklahoma-Kansas area, but in the end he was to lose after a "brisk fight" to L. A. Wilson, a farmer from El Reno, Oklahoma. He accepted defeat with the same grace as he had all the successes he had enjoyed.[36] But Phillips was a man of destiny; the future would be kind to him.

Patience and additional recognition through the years ultimately produced the coveted seat on the regional Federal Reserve Board. A vacancy on the Board occurred in 1926. On December 3, he was the only candidate for the position, having been endorsed unanimously by all the major clearing houses in the district.

He accepted with the humility of an Iowa farm boy, saying that he had no preconceived ideas of his importance. He added: "I hope to supply information on the oil industry to the directors . . . that will be helpful in determining policies of benefit to the industry. Throughout the country oil is still looked upon as a game; as a highly speculative industry instead of the well-grounded, essential business that it is, and even bankers can well afford to pursue their studies further."[37] L. E. Phillips would serve without interruption on the Kansas City regional directorate until his death in 1944. It was a responsibility he relished, and he coveted the honor more than any other he ever received. His reelection in subsequent years reflected the esteem and respect which his banking associates held for him.[38]

Such recognition was a fitting tribute to a man who loved the banking profession and through it brought prestige and recognition to his city, state, and nation. There is a persistent story that L. E. and Frank, when they began their early careers in the Indian Territory, actually had embarked on a dream of establishing and directing a "string of banks" from Bartlesville to Kansas City. In this dream they were influenced strongly by John Gibson, Frank's father-in-law, who was himself a successful banker. The long list of directorships that both L. E. and Frank held in banks throughout the Midwestern states unquestionably attests in part to their earliest goal, but it also speaks dramatically to the powerful economic and political influence of the Phillips Petroleum Company.

Of the many legacies of the lives of the Phillips brothers in Oklahoma, one of the greatest was their influence in the development of banking, and L. E. was the brother whose impact was felt more dramatically.

4

FAMILY YEARS IN BARTLESVILLE
1905-1929

Lee Eldas Phillips might be characterized in many ways. He was, despite his workaholic tendencies, first and foremost a family man, although he was obliged to spend much time away from them because of business responsibilities. Frail from youth, his precarious health at times humbled him when his wealth projected him into seemingly limitless activities. It was in 1910, when he was forced to spend time for health reasons at the Battle Creek Sanitarium, that he penned some of his most poignant thoughts. As a part of a Thanksgiving Day celebration, he was asked to "write one sentence, that for which you are most thankful today." His response was: "Good health, an ideal wife and family and hosts of friends."[1]

"An ideal wife and family and hosts of friends" were the substance of this great man's life. From the time he emerged from Western Normal College, he had fixed his eyes on Lenora Carr, a friend and sweetheart from his childhood. Node, as he called her, was in no hurry to marry, preferring not to relinquish her life as a father's girl too quickly. To make matters more difficult, her father was none too eager for her to wed Lee Eldas, who seemed destined to be a rural school teacher for the rest of his career.

On the other hand, L. E. had been taught by his father not to take on the responsibilities of a wife until he could adequately provide for her. Following that ad-

Early Bartlesville, showing north end of Delaware Street.

vice, he delayed serious consideration of marriage until some semblance of economic stability emerged. Quietly during his years with George B. Rex and Son, he patiently wooed Node, often writing letters to her which Eva, Node's sister and postmistress of Bedford, concealed in her clothing and brought home to her older sister to avoid father Carr's displeasure.[2]

But the time arrived and blessings were secured. L. E. and Node were married in November of 1902 and moved to Knoxville, Iowa, to start their home. Both were 26 years old at the time. Two sons, Philip Rex in 1903 and Lee Eldas, Jr., in 1905, were born to them in Knoxville before they moved in September of 1905 to Bartlesville in the Indian Territory. Their third child, a daughter named Martha Jane, was born on November 27, 1906, before Oklahoma was admitted to the Union, and her brothers through the years would tease her about not having been born in the United States.[3]

Their first home was on Delaware Street, which they occupied until L. E. had a new home constructed at 507 Cherokee in 1907. They were to enjoy that residence until 1922 when L. E. purchased a larger brick home at 1201 Cherokee, located across the street from brother

Johnstone and Keeler General Store on Second Street, in early Bartlesville where the Phillips bought necessities.

Frank's beautiful mansion. In time, L. E. would add significantly to the house, and it became one of the "show places" in the city, one of elegant appointments and comfortable accommodations. It was spacious enough to provide for large entertainments, but private enough to allow a loving family to share their lives in convenient and quiet seclusion. The Phillips home was always open to their friends, who were urged to share it either on an impromptu or invited basis.

Most of the children's formative years were spent at 507 Cherokee, a two-story frame house with a large roofed front porch. Awnings sheltered the windows and porch from the sun, and a brick sidewalk provided protected walkways during inclement weather. It was a comfortable house, built large enough to accommodate the five family members. There was a small frame house for the servants, who helped Node with housework and child rearing. Nothing of great excitement punctuated the early family years in that comfortable house.[4]

One incident of special interest occurred in September of 1909 when red ants "over-ran" the Cherokee residence. L. E. appealed through the local press for assistance from anyone who had successfully dealt with

Phillips first Bartlesville residence on Delaware Street, where Martha Jane Phillips was born.

the problem, giving his phone number as a convenience. So overwhelming were the telephone responses that the family not only was obliged to take the phone off the hook but also to ask the telephone company to tell other erstwhile callers that their phone was out of order. L. E. commented in despair: "The next time I ask for a remedy for red ants, I am going to explain to the obliging newspaper reporter that I do not want the general public to make any suggestions."[5]

From the photograph albums which L. E. kept, it is obvious that the Phillips couple were closely knit and that the children occupied their loving attention. Unidentified newspaper clippings tell of childhood illnesses and of at least one serious accident to Philip which resulted in a broken collarbone. One picture, so typical of children at an early age, shows the three children at play in the yard with Phil pulling Martha Jane in a wagon and L. E., Jr., sitting in a small wheelbarrow. Theirs was a normal childhood, and as they grew up they entered the Bartlesville public schools.

The Phillips children at play at 507 Cherokee Street, their second home in Bartlesville.

Remembering how he cherished trips to the home of his grandparents, L. E. frequently took the children to Iowa, even allowing Node and the young ones to remain for a time when business summoned him back to Bartlesville.[6] And because Node's health worsened in the years following the birth of their children, L. E. encouraged her to take their young family to Colorado for the summer months; she and the children actually lived in Denver during the years 1913-15. She was born with a heart condition that always improved by cooler climates.[7] Despite this affliction and the concern it caused her family, she lived to be 90.

Disciplining the children was principally Node's responsibility, for L. E. usually left for work at 7:00 a.m. and sometimes did not return until well after they were in bed. Phil remembers in the early years that he "knew his father only on Sundays," because that was the only day he permitted himself to be away from his business responsibilities. Sunday was church day, and L. E. and Node seldom missed a service. Their children would

Lenora convalescing at Battle Creek Sanitarium in 1910.

remain staunch churchgoers throughout their lives. In what time he had with them and in his loving and mature way, L. E. trained his children by direction. He required his children to work for an allowance of 25 cents per week, for which the boys had to mow the lawn and wash and grease the car. The money was not given without some additional direction. Each was permitted to spend a nickel on a movie, purchase a candy bar with another nickel, contribute a nickel at church, and deposit a dime in a savings account. Phil's savings account number, which still holds, is 15, one of the earliest accounts on record. With such persistent supervision and encouragement, L. E. did not need to use the rod in disciplining his children.

Neither did Node, who never raised her hand to any of the children. When they behaved badly, she explained to them that they were ill and needed medicine. Rather than spank them, she administered liberal doses of caster oil, which not only "cured their illnesses" but also markedly improved their dispositions. Phil remembers this effective method of disciplining vividly. Once while

The Phillips children in 1909.

in Colorado Springs, Node took the children by streetcar to a local park. Phil teased Martha Jane to the point of tears and, when they arrived at the park, Node immediately took Phil on a return trip aboard the car to their residence, gave him a large tablespoon of the horrible liquid, and returned with him to enjoy the picnic lunch she had prepared. Phil does not recall enjoying the meal, but is certain that the others did—some of it at his expense.[8]

Phil grew to be a strapping boy and played football as an end on the Bartlesville High School team. L. E., Jr., was thin, although strong, but was too small for competitive sports. Martha Jane grew into a petite and beautiful girl who studied music and was feature editor for the high school newspaper. All of them were active in drama productions, and all were popular during their respective years in high school. Phil and L. E., Jr., also were active in Boy Scouts.[9]

Because education had been so important to both L. E. and Node, they insisted on advanced educations for

L.E. with his children, Phil, L.E., Jr., and Martha Jane in 1914.

their children. When Phil graduated from BHS in May 1922, he matriculated at the University of Kansas. Following his graduation in 1926, he joined a University World Cruise, which combined instruction with sightseeing on a round-the-world trip which lasted eight months.[10]

Lee, Jr., also enrolled at the University of Kansas following his graduation from Bartlesville High in 1923, and despite the fact that he always had lamented being too small, he became a member of the KU boxing team. He graduated from the University in 1927, and he then likewise went on a world tour on February 5, 1928.[11]

L.E.'s first automobile, a 1914 Overland, shown here in Denver, Colorado, in July, 1914, where Mrs. Phillips was residing for her health.

Meanwhile, Martha Jane graduated from BHS in 1925, winning medals in history and domestic arts and earning honorable mention in English. Later she entered Erskine School in Boston.[12]

The children's college years were good ones for L. E. and Node. The boys came home at holiday seasons, and the Phillips entertained them and their friends with dinners and dances. During the summer, L. E. encouraged both boys to spend their vacations working on Uncle Waite's magnificent and beautiful ranch in New Mexico. This ranch, known as Philmont, later was to be given to the Boy Scouts of America, an organization which both Phil and L. E., Jr., enjoyed as young boys. Martha Jane, during her summer vacations, did the thing young ladies did then, entertaining her friends at home or traveling to Iowa or Tulsa to visit grandparents and relatives.[13]

When the opportunity came to travel abroad, L. E. and Node took such of the children as were available to accompany them. In 1921, following an American Bankers Association meeting in Los Angeles, L. E., Node, and

Martha Jane spent a few weeks in Hawaii. After Philip graduated from high school in 1922, the entire family spent the three summer months in Europe together.

Traveling, to Lee and Node, was a sharing experience. They enjoyed being together on long trips, especially sea voyages, because it allowed both to relax and rest their frail bodies. After Martha Jane was born, Node often was obliged to spend several months each year away from Bartlesville, either in residence in Colorado or at medical centers in Kansas City or Battle Creek, Michigan. She had palpitations of the heart, so bad at times that her family as well as her physicians feared for her life. Little wonder that L. E. was willing to endure the loneliness of separation; although it was quite expensive at times, it was no sacrifice of consequence for a man who loved his wife so deeply. They made up for their separations by planning long vacations to exotic parts of the world.

His affection for her and his concern for her health resulted once in an alteration of L. E.'s steadfast rule against flying. Although the Phillips Petroleum Company had owned an airplane from the days of the old Ford Tri-Motor, Lee Eldas always traveled by surface transportation. However, during one of her trips to Waite Phillips' New Mexico ranch, Node suffered severe palpitations and seemed to be hovering near death. Waite called L. E., who agreed under the circumstances to charter a Lockheed aircraft to fly to her bedside. Fortunately, Node's condition improved, and L. E. rode the train back to Bartlesville.[14]

L. E.'s love for Node was spiritual and physical. She was a beautiful woman at heart and in appearance. "She had deep blue eyes that twinkled most of the time because she was happy." Her skin was fair and clear, and her hair had a slight natural curl. She was slender and willowy, moving about gracefully. She had a splendid sense of humor and did things to make others happy.

L.E. and Lenora in 1926.

She was appreciative of the things L. E. bought her, but she infrequently wore the expensive jewelry which he gave her as special gifts, feeling that the pieces were too showy. She seldom argued with her husband, preferring instead to support him in any decision he chose to make. She disliked keeping him waiting because she knew it irritated him and aggravated his high blood pressure.[15]

During one of their periods of separation, when she was in Kansas City for treatment and he was in the Texas Panhandle on business, L. E. sent her two telegrams which in their way, despite the public nature of the medium, openly expressed his affection for her:

> April 28, 1926: . . . am very sorry not to be with you on your birthday. I hope you like the flowers and everything that may be intended for you as an expression of my love . . . .

> April 29, 1926: . . . hope you like the pearls each of which represent a year of pleasant memory spent with you. Do not mind the cost since you earned them

. . . . Just keep working to get fat and keep on loving
me and I will be happy . . . .[16]

And that after 24 years of marriage! But as Will Rogers,
an infrequent guest in the Phillips home, once remarked, "One thing I admire about you Phillips men is
that you are still with the same wives you started with
early in life."[17]

Even before the Phillips moved to 1201 Cherokee,
they were becoming socially active in the community. L.
E. would entertain his colleagues in the Commercial
Club or host a whist party for his friends. Node entertained at bridge parties, scheduling them during the
morning hours in order to avoid the heat of summer
afternoons. At Christmas time or on other special oc-
casions, they would host what had by then become a
circle of "polite society" friends, a circle which included
the best families in Bartlesville. They also used the Hillcrest Country Club for many of their social functions.

L. E. was not a musician; in fact, one of his friends
once joked, "There was quite an accident out at the
country club the other night. L. E. tried to sing." Lee
admitted that he did not know much about music but
liked the sound of it. "It soothes a man," he once remarked, but concluded, "I don't know one note from
another, except promissory notes."[18] Yet he knew of
Node's love for and training in music, and he purchased
and installed an expensive pipe organ in their home in
1926. It was a magnificent addition to 1201 Cherokee
Street and to the entire community. A formal dedication
was held, complete with visiting celebrities from Chicago
and Kansas City, who delivered a special musicale for
a group of selected guests. Thereafter, Node treated her
friends to occasional musicales whenever there was a
slack period in other social activities in the city.[19]

Node was a fortunate woman and she knew it. She
returned L. E.'s love and gave him wifely support in all

his busy activities. L. E. was extroverted and needed her patient understanding. Phil, their oldest son, does not recall that either spoke harshly to the other or that they carried their disagreements on their coat sleeves. Whatever L. E. wanted to do and when he wanted to do it were fine with Node. She would pick up her needlepoint materials and accompany him at any time, even if it meant remaining isolated in a hotel room for days. Theirs was a rare relationship.

Another enviable relationship existed between L. E. and Frank. The harmony which existed between these two defies the normal behavior between brothers, and it was wholesome to see them as "best friends," close confidants in personal matters, and frequent visitors in each other's homes. Neither seemed to threaten the other's ego despite occasional differences of opinion. As talented as he was, Lee Eldas Phillips assumed and accepted his role as vice president in every joint venture he undertook with his brother. Once when teased about this fact, he responded by saying that Frank was the eldest, and it was his right to be president if he chose.[20] And Frank always did, even in the banking firms they developed, despite the fact that L. E. was the decision maker and manager of those operations.

The fact that Frank seemed always to receive first credit for each accomplishment they enjoyed apparently was of little consequence to L. E. Both brothers had tremendous respect for each other. Each was the other's confidant, each the other's complement. Frank was slightly introverted, L. E. outgoing and gregarious. Frank was the adroit businessman and financier, Lee the deft personnel handler and operations manager. Frank frequently was in New York where they maintained a corporate office; L. E. most often was in Bartlesville running the business. They made an enviable and inseparable team, their blood relationship cementing their trust in ways that few management teams ever experi-

Japanese gardens at 1201 Cherokee Street, the Phillips third and last home in Bartlesville.

ence. This fact may well have been the greatest asset the Phillips Petroleum Company ever enjoyed. And L. E., as manager, was unquestionably of immense value to the firm he helped co-found.[21]

Lee's personality was such that he "never met a stranger." As Phil put it, "If he left Bartlesville on a train headed for Los Angeles, he would know every person aboard on a first-name basis by the time the train arrived at its destination." But unlike his friend Will Rogers, L. E. did know one man whom he did not like: John L. Lewis, the union boss whose wage demands for mine workers in 1904 had brought bankruptcy to the old Hawkeye Coal Mine in Knoxville, Iowa. He never forgave Lewis for contributing to that failure.[22]

Philosophically, Lee Eldas was conservative, although he later would urge greater governmental regulation of the oil industry. He did not believe in credit, insisting that his family pay cash for everything, yet he

Lenora with Mrs. Frank (Jane) Phillips, her sister-in-law, entertainng at 1201 Cherokee Street.

was a willing partner in Frank's efforts to borrow huge sums in order to finance their oil operations. Once during the depression, when Phillips Petroleum desperately needed additional financing in order to remain in business, L. E. waited long hours by the telephone for news of Frank's New York transactions, all the while fearing he would not succeed. When the call finally came and the news was positive, Lee went into a gleeful dance.[23]

His personal philosophies were simple yet profound. Once while speaking to a graduating class at the University of Tulsa, he outlined a simple code: "Be true to yourself, loyal to your fellowmen, faithful to your God."[24] To these, throughout his life, he added numerous tenets: strive hard, be self-reliant, honor your parents, respect your heritage, and have a sense of humor.

Humor was integral to his personality. Typical of his lighthearted pokes at social customs, he once offered

the following recipe to the women in Bartlesville who
desired beautiful complexions:

> Go to the drug store and buy a choice assortment of
> paints, powders, skin foods, enamels and beauty lo-
> tions; and carry it three miles from the house and
> bury it in a secret place, then every morning before
> breakfast take a walk to see if anyone has disturbed
> the cache.[25]

Although he frequently felt weak and worn out, he was
known to start his days jokingly with statements such as,
"If I felt any better this morning, I would have to take
something for it."[26] Still he was a frequent visitor to a
Kansas City Clinic and an occasional resident patient at
the Battle Creek Sanitarium.

His chief affliction was high blood pressure, which
no doubt was aggravated by excessive cigarette smoking.
He also suffered periodically from a gastro-intestinal
ailment, probably diverticulitis, which sapped his appetite and left him weak. Special diets at the Battle Creek
Sanitarium did wonders for his intestinal difficulties, but
his refusal to slow down in work habits and put aside
his cigarettes only increased his problems with high
blood pressure. His decision to travel and to take long
vacations undoubtedly was an effort to achieve a change
of pace and alleviate tensions.

He enjoyed a good story, but was not known to repeat
"dirty jokes." Because he had once been a traveling salesman, he was almost addicted to the utilization of that
setting for his funny stories. One of his favorite tales
involved the proverbial traveling salesman and farmer's
daughter. While traveling through the country, the salesman was forced by high waters to seek refuge at a
farmer's house for an evening. The next morning he
discovered the farmer's beautiful daughter and, under
the guise of getting her into his room, he asked her to

join him at his bedroom window. He pointed to an object in the water. "Tell me," he said, "what is that hat doing down there, going back and forth in the water instead of swirling around?"

"Oh," she replied, "that's Grandpa. He was so busy with the harvest that he allowed the grass to grow too tall, and he said yesterday that come hell or high water he was going to mow the lawn today." After telling the joke, L. E. would laugh and say, "Now see; my jokes aren't dirty; it all depends on where your mind is."[27]

L. E. balanced his life with healthy portions of appreciation for his ancestry and heritage. Returning to his Iowa moorings was one of his most enjoyable and most frequent luxuries, even after he became a millionaire. Countless times he returned to Conway, or Creston, or Bedford, or Knoxville or even Des Moines where some of his closest friends still resided. He wanted his young children to know about their father's heritage, and he took them as often as he could. His trip in October of 1937 was liberally documented by photographs of those places where precious childhood memories originated, and his annotations of these in his photo albums represent some of the most detailed and accurate recordings that he left. But then, those were the cobblestones he felt compelled to mark for posterity.[28]

On one of his trips to Conway he discovered that the old church which Node and her parents had attended was being torn down, thus threatening to erase one important vestige of his family's heritage. He promptly obtained the old pulpit and the church bell and had them shipped to Bartlesville. The bell, although for a time at Woolaroc, Frank's rustic ranch home, was later moved to L. E.'s farm.[29]

The bell reflected another important facet of his life. Although raised a Methodist, he chose to accept baptism into the First Christian Church in order that his family could be united in worship. He was respected by his ministers, even when he closed his eyes during sermons, because L. E. could always surprise them later by asking a substantive question about the meaning of some part of the morning's message. He became a deacon and eventually chairman of the board for his church, and he proved a generous contributor, not only in weekly pledges but in more costly church renovation as well. He also bought the parsonage used by the church. Moreover, he contributed $25,000 in installments to a national Christian Church drive.[30]

Church leaders respected him highly and were quick to rejoice with him whenever a new honor or accomplishment occurred. Annually at Christmas time he received a carefully thought out message from Dr. Harry L. Ice, minister of the First Christian Church of Bartlesville, whom L. E. had once surprised with the gift of a Ford automobile.[31]

Lee, on occasion, considered entering politics, and his name was mentioned periodically as an apt candidate for governor. Oklahoma was not then ready for a Republican governor, and L. E. was quite aware of that fact. He also was mentioned by friends as a candidate worthy for local office, but he managed to sidestep any efforts to draft him into that endeavor. Twice he strongly considered running for the U. S. Senate, once with the apparent blessings of President Herbert Hoover, but his entry into the race was not crowned with success.[32]

The most important effort made to attract him into politics came to light only shortly before his death. General Patrick Hurley, a long-time friend, as well as a member of Hoover's cabinet, almost persuaded Lee Eldas to accept the governor generalship of the Philippines, but he declined the appointment. ˙He confided to his son Phil several times that he would have loved to have taken the position, but simply did not want to leave the Phillips Petroleum Company or his orderly life in Bartlesville.[33]

As the company grew in size and organizational sta-

The Phillips family arriving in Honolulu in July, 1926, for a vacation.

bility, L. E. found time to pursue his hobbies. He loved to travel, and on trips to major cities he always enjoyed cinema and stage productions. He loved the Ziegfeld Follies and other musicals, which Node also relished. He enjoyed fishing and managed to work in a major camping trip with friends almost every year. He loved golf, was a bogey player, and once held the "call shot" title at the Hillcrest Country Club. And when his workload precluded travel, he would quietly seek solace at his nearby farm, where he raised registered hogs and where he could rest without interruption because he refused to have a telephone installed. "If they want me," he would say, "they can just drive out and get me."[34]

Hardly a hobby but a very enjoyable diversion was the relationships he had with friends. Frequently his friends were invited to share evenings either at the Cherokee Street residence or at the farm. When the Phillips left on one of their many ocean voyages, those same friends flooded them with telegrams expressing good wishes for a rewarding trip. These friendships had many other expressions. The following letter evidences the genuine, heartfelt relationships L. E. developed. Written to L. E. in red pencil by Nobe Welty at Christmas in 1928, it began,

> Yes, there is a Santa Claus, and I, like you, think he must be God.
>
> However God is hard for us to comprehend, but friends like you and your wonderful wife are near enough to be more easy to comprehend. So, my faith is strengthened by having friends, and friends like you and Nora are not so common that we can afford to fail to appreciate them.
>
> Maybe you'll understand this red letter. The red signifies that this appreciation is verbally of my heart's blood.[35]

Another friend and annual letter writer at Christmas was H. H. McClintock. Always his letters sought to express admiration and appreciation for a true friend, Lee Eldas Phillips. One of these letters, dated December 25, 1925, was a reflective piece about growing old and about the enjoyment of being Santa Claus to loved ones. But, mused McClintock, "we no longer have any children in our homes." They were growing up and doing their own thinking, just as every new generation will. Soon the young would leave to build for their own families, thus causing parents to slowly slip "into that period of being 'old folks'."[36]

His message was prophetic and timely. L. E. was increasingly aware that his children were growing older; at that time all of them were college students and increasingly drawn away from Bartlesville. Soon it would be just L. E. and Node, with that difficult task of adjusting to an empty nest. Yet they faced this future with a growing love that was limitless and eternal. They were better prepared than most couples to watch their children launch out into their mature lives.

H. H. McClintock certainly recognized that fact. This further quote from the letter of December, 1925 indelibly reflects the influence L. E. had on others:

> It is not every one who enjoys the blessings of a family or knows how to make such an end possible. I am sure it is all in how one "grows" that family. Like a tree, the more proper the care, the better will be the fruit. I am always attracted to this side of your's and Nora's good sense and wise judgement. You could have made a terrible mess of the job; most "rich" people do. But the fruit bespeaks the care in pruning and I know the joy that is yours to have your family circle about you again. It is the more increased because of the pride you feel from knowing that your ideals have been quite satisfactorily reached in the character of your "youngsters." And what can bring greater joy than this?[37]

What indeed! And nothing but pride and happiness attended the departure of their children. Phil, after returning in 1927 from his University World Cruise, joined the production department of Phillips Petroleum Company. L. E. wanted Phil to learn the oil business from "the ground up," and after several intermediary stops, Phil was eventually assigned to manage the Springfield, Illinois, district. Still later he would enter the Navy as an aerial gunnery instructor and see service in Hawaii.[38]

The year 1929 was also important for the Phillips. Aside from the fact that the nation suffered the beginnings of its worst depression, the year was a joyous one for two important reasons: both L. E., Jr., and Martha Jane announced their engagements and were married before year's end. The University of Kansas played cupid for the two couples. While Lee, Jr., was a student there in 1926, he met and courted Anne Katherine Innes, daughter of Walter P. Innes of Wichita, Kansas, who was one of the wealthiest and most prominent retail businessmen in the Southwest. Their engagement was announced on August 11, 1929, and it greatly pleased L. E. Phillips, Sr.[39]

Hardly had that engagement become known when Martha Jane on August 16 announced her plans to marry Wilbur "Twink" Starr of Hutchinson, Kansas, a heralded football star on the University of Kansas team. The two had met at a fraternity dance at the University. Martha Jane was at home at the time from Erskine School in Boston, and was visiting with Lee, Jr., at the University. It was "love at first sight" for both Martha Jane and Twink, but neither realized the seriousness of their feelings for a time. In order to maintain his contact with and pursuit of Martha Jane, Twink joined the Phillips Petroleum Company following his graduation, moved to Bartlesville, and eventually won her hand after a two-year courtship.[40]

The marriage ceremonies were elaborate social events, reflecting both the prominence of the families as well as the genuine love they felt for their children. Martha Jane's wedding occurred on October 26, 1929, at the First Christian Church in Bartlesville. She was given in marriage by her proud father, and both Phil and Lee, Jr., as well as his betrothed, Anne Katherine Innes, were attendants. In turn, L. E., Jr.'s, marriage took place at the Innes' residence in Wichita, Kansas, on November 26, 1929, with Phil serving his brother as best man, and the newly married Wilbur and Martha Jane Starr as attendants to the wedding party.[41]

Thus did Lee Eldas and Lenora Phillips' lives take an inevitable turn. They rejoiced as Martha Jane and Wilbur honeymooned in Havana and returned to live in Bartlesville. And they happily watched while Lee, Jr., and Anne Katherine left on a wedding trip to Hawaii and returned to a temporary home in nearby Oklahoma City. Ultimately the Starrs would settle in Kansas City, the Lee Phillips, Jr., in Wichita. And although they tended to scatter in establishing permanent homesites, the children and their parents were never separated in spirit. They were as close as the telephone or the telegraph office, both of which they used frequently to communicate with each other. And they were frequent visitors in each other's homes.[42]

Depression clouds hovered ominously over the Phillips Petroleum Company as the weddings passed into history, and L. E. and Frank shouldered increasing pressure and responsibility in keeping their great company solvent and productive. They met this challenge with the same faith and confidence they had relied upon in the other difficult situations they had faced since 1904 when the old Hawkeye Coal Company had closed. That they and their company survived the depression when many of their contemporaries did not is but another reflection of the "destiny" that was theirs. They would be required to paint a few more cobblestones on their way to the summit.

5

OILMAN: THE EARLY YEARS
OF PHILLIPS PETROLEUM
1917-1925

Leaving the banking business for oil exploration, although he truly loved banking, was not difficult for L. E. Phillips; it was just another cobblestone which needed marking. As a banker for many years, L. E. felt he had "paid his dues"; he had worked long hours and, with patience, had fashioned a powerful financial institution out of three smaller enterprises. But over those same years, L. E.'s role had changed from chief bookkeeper to general manager; much of what he had done earlier was now delegated to subordinates who routinely conducted the business and developed financial reports which reduced much of the decision making process to mere mechanics. Not that the challenge was gone from banking; it was simply that a greater challenge beckoned when Frank urgently appealed to him to use his talents in helping to develop their fledgling oil empire.[1]

L. E. was no novice to the oil game. His earliest experiences in Bartlesville were in petroleum exploration. In the beginning it was said of the two brothers that L. E. spent his time scouting for well sites, and Frank worked out the details for drilling them. After the brothers left the banking business to devote full-time to their oil holdings, this pattern of shared responsibilities continued, but on a grander scale. Arranging financial packages for drilling, building storage tanks, and laying pipelines required frequent trips to New York City

78

money markets.² Frank remained the financier and utilized the corporate office in New York for raising needed capital, leaving L. E. to run the business in Bartlesville and secure lease rights for expanded operations. Moreover, L. E. knew the petulancy of the oil business, having kept the books and paid the bills during "boom and bust." Having Frank assume the difficult tasks of President and chief fund raiser suited L. E. perfectly. As a banker, he knew only too well that few of his banking constituents understood or had full appreciation for the volatile petroleum industry. The price of crude fluctuated wildly, often soaring to high prices per barrel, then just as suddenly plummeting rapidly whenever a new field opened and flooded the market. Thus oil in storage tanks always had uncertain value, and few local bankers would risk their assets on such a vacillating commodity.³

L. E. and Frank, not unlike their brother Waite in Tulsa, were fortunate to own banks which could underwrite some of their operations, but all too quickly the costs of meeting competition in an industry changing with new technological developments required capital which could only be secured in the quantities needed in larger financial centers. Perhaps for that principal reason, the Phillips brothers decided in the summer of 1917 to merge all their holdings. They offered for public sale 100,000 shares of common stock, as well as $1.5 million in preferred stock in the Phillips Petroleum Company, a new corporation founded on June 13, 1917, under Delaware laws.

At the time of the merger, the Phillips Petroleum assets were approximately three million dollars. There were 27 employees and an array of leases, producing wells, and equipment scattered throughout Oklahoma and Kansas. Two corporations were absorbed, the Lewcinda Oil and Standish Oil companies, which still produced oil from the old Osage leases that had remained

When the Phillips brothers sold their oil holdings in 1915-16, federal regulations forbade the transfer of Lease 185, Burbank Field, to the Tidal Oil Company. Later at this site, the Phillips reentered the oil business with great success.

in the Phillips' portfolio when they attempted to liquidate their holdings in 1915-1916. In all, the new corporation listed 57,423 acres, located in Oklahoma and Kansas, on which there were 108 producing wells. The merged companies had 12 rigs in operation on some of the undeveloped leases, two of which were at work in Cowley County, Kansas, just south of the Augusta field in Butler County. Several others were drilling on the Osage lands near Bartlesville. The officers of the new corporation were: Frank Phillips, president; L. E. Phillips, vice president; and Henry E. Koopman, a long-time associate of Frank's, secretary-treasurer.[4]

Lee surprised banking circles in Oklahoma when he retired in 1919 from active management of the Bartlesville National Bank, one of the eight largest financial institutions in the state. But his move in 1919 mirrored to the public the increasing size and growing importance of the Phillips Petroleum Company, ·a corporation by then operating in Kansas, Oklahoma, Texas, and Kentucky. And if any believed the move was distasteful, L. E. dispelled the notion by stating publicly on May 20, 1919, that he liked the oil business. He further commented that he was "becoming weaned away from the banking business more rapidly than he supposed possible."⁵

From its founding in 1917, Phillips Petroleum plunged headlong into the rough-and-tumble environment which characterized the oil business in Oklahoma. Oil leases in the Osage lands after 1916 only could be obtained during public auctions which were held in Pawhuska, oddly enough with bidders sitting on the ground under a tree which came to be known as the "Million Dollar Elm." Because the bidding was always spirited, a clever and knowledgable auctioneer, Colonel E. Walters, kept the action quite competitive among the likes of Bill Skelly, E. W. Marland, and the Phillips brothers. One story Frank delighted in telling about L. E. occurred when the two brothers were sitting on the ground under that old elm while Walters was striving to drive the bid for one lease up another $100,000. He encountered some difficulty and was on the verge of "hammering down" the last bid when L. E. apparently gestured an offer for the higher price—which Walters promptly accepted and closed out the bidding.

Later, it was learned—or at least Frank persistently led others to believe—that L. E. actually had not bid on the lease at all, but rather had merely taken a healthy swat at a fly which had been flying around his hat for a frustratingly long time. L. E. Fitzgarrald, a long-time

The "Million Dollar Elm" at the Pawhuska Indian Agency, under which numerous bidding wars for Osage Indian leaseholds were waged.

Phillips employee, remembers that the story circulated for years thereafter; the most gleeful repeater was Frank Phillips, who always recalled that "L. E. cost the company $100,000 because he couldn't stand the flies" at the old Pawhuska Agency's auction site.[6]

By 1920, the growing activities of the new firm were chronicled increasingly in the press. On April 15 that year it was reported that a well in the Osage tract was completed and was "gushing" naturally at 500 barrels an hour, the "biggest well ever drilled in the Osage." Magnificent though it was, the well site had been the subject of a larger story on February 4, 1920, when Phillips purchased the leasehold for $220,000, an enormous investment at the time. Such a price merely indicated how competitive oil speculation had become. As was the custom that year, auctions for Osage lands were held in a movie house in Pawhuska, and representatives of the Phillips, Marland, and Gilliland companies, among others, had gathered to bid on the best lots. At the February

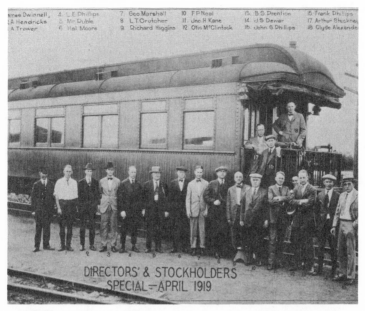

The Second Annual Directors Meeting of the Phillips Petroleum Company in April, 1919.

sale, the Osage Indians realized a total of $3,102,700 from the sale of lease rights to 31,773 acres. Phillips' bid of $220,000 was the highest at that auction.[7]

As the clamor for the better lands mounted, bidding soared still higher. Ten new tracts were auctioned on April 4, 1921, bringing the unbelievable sum of $7,577,000. Phillips acquired one at $1,005,000, but it was not the highest price paid, that dubious distinction falling to Waite Phillips, who paid $1,325,000 for a choice tract on the western edge of the proven Burbank field. In December that year, L. E. Phillips paid $663,000 for Tract 36 in the Osage lands, but was outbid for two other tracts by the Prairie Oil and Gas Company, which paid $800,000 and $700,000, respectively, for the leases.[8]

"It is perfectly ridiculous," L. E. fumed, "the amount paid for these leases." Perhaps so, but the expanded

Burbank field was a lucrative investment for successful bidders. If the price of leases truly worried L. E., the net affect on the company earnings and growth was anything but negative. During 1921, construction of four 55,000-barrel steel storage tanks was begun in the Slick field near Cushing, the Phillips Company apparently being "intent upon storing its output to take advantage of a higher crude market, *its large financial resources enabling it to do so* [italics supplied]."[9] New records were being set at Phillips Petroleum; gross oil production at the end of 1921 was averaging 17,000 barrels per day from some 900 wells on 130 separate properties, as compared to 108 producers at the time of incorporation in 1917.

Additionally, corporate earnings not only were good but projected profits promised even more. Statistics for the third quarter of 1921 showed a net return, after taxes and company expenditures, of $800,000, with an anticipated $1.3 million net for the entire year. These figures reflected an earnings ratio of between six and seven dollars per share of outstanding stock. At year's end, the Phillips Petroleum Company declared its initial quarterly dividend of fifty cents per share.[10]

Perhaps what concerned L. E. most was, again, the volatile nature of the oil industry. Even in the year 1921, there were periods of hard times. In June, the Gilliland Oil Company of Tulsa was forced into receivership when it became "entangled in financial difficulties." Oil was bringing only one dollar per barrel, an insufficient price to permit John H. Gilliland to cope with his overwhelming indebtedness. Then in August, W. H. Gray, president of the National Association of Independent Oil Men, warned that it might become necessary to limit, even shut down, production until the price of crude rose. "Oklahoma," he declared, "is producing too much oil for the general good of the industry."[11]

Lee Eldas agreed. He was aware of proration by large

petroleum producers throughout the country, especially
in some states where crude was bringing only fifty cents
per barrel. He pledged that the Phillips Petroleum Company would cooperate to the limit, even to supporting
a complete shutdown if it became necessary.[12] Little wonder that L. E. would deplore the rising costs of "doing
business," or that he would encourage the construction
of storage tanks so that some production could be with-
held from the market until prices improved.

The slowdown hurt all companies, even the Phillips
Company, which still was in a solid financial status. But
even in hard times, the Phillips brothers did not lose
their sense of humor. During a visit to New York City
with one of their vice presidents, M. M. Doan, Frank
playfully challenged the two (L. E. and Doan) to a game
of pitch. Since he feared there would not be enough
work to keep them all busy for the year, he stated that
the loser of the game would be obliged to return to
Bartlesville and manage the affairs of the company while
the other two vacationed in Europe for the rest of the
year. Continuing the ruse, both L. E. and Doan declined,
stating that if all went back, each could anticipate at least
a short vacation. Otherwise the loser would be "up to his
eyes" in work throughout the year.[13]

Hard times, to be sure, but the situation was to ease
by November, at least in Oklahoma: oil prices rose to
two dollars per barrel.[14] And at Pawhuska in March of
1922, bidding wars produced a sale that broke all previous records. Frank Phillips, representing both the Phillips Petroleum and Skelly Oil companies, paid $1,335,000
for Tract 23 in the expanding Burbank field. "It makes
us a bit dizzy," a newsman wrote, "when we consider the
price the Phillips-Skelly interests paid for two quarter
section leases in the Burbank pool."[15] But, to paraphrase
a famous comedian, "he hadn't seen anything yet."

By June of 1922 the "old" records had been shattered
again. During the bidding for new Burbank leases, the

Gypsy Oil Company paid $1.6 million for one 160-acre tract, barely topping the Phillips-Skelly purchase of another for $1,585,000. News of these sales spread rapidly, and the reporting bordered on sensationalism. News analysts had predicted, because of "the tight money market," that the bidding might be much softer than at previous auctions. But after analyzing the actual sales results, a record $10,887,950 had been "hammered down on the block in the Constantine theatre" for oil leases. "Pretty good land the Osage Indians own down here, isn't it," one reporter quipped. That represented "a little bonus of about $5,000 apiece" to each Osage Indian headright, the journalist continued, making the average family of four "exactly $20,000 richer as a result of white man's frenzied chewing of cigars." And he concluded that the Osages might be moved to ask, "Mebbe we ought to set 'em up in cigars again, huh?"[16]

Frank represented the Phillips Company at most of these auctions, and his actions were characterized by a quiet boldness. He made his bids calmly, even those which topped the million dollar level, and he was imperturbed when competitors overbid him. Many bystanders were amazed when, with the raising of an eyebrow, or the flicking of Phillips' ever-present cigar, an auctioneer would promptly respond to one of Frank's offerings. But sometimes it fell to L. E. to be the spokesman for the company at Pawhuska, and by 1922 he seemed equally as unemotional when he was forced to make an offer in excess of a million dollars for a lease right. Such consistency in performance by both brothers, in meeting the competition for new acreage, is evidence again that they were in close consultation and in full accord regarding what was best for the Phillips Petroleum Company, even when they were sharing a bidding venture with other companies. The two men, at times, were referred to in the press as acting on behalf of "Phillips and others"; the "others" most often meant

Skelly Oil with which Phillips worked on numerous leases. But the brothers also infrequently represented their younger brother, Waite, whose Tulsa-based company was growing rapidly in stature.[17]

By mid-1922, the Phillips Petroleum Company had made significant new progress. It was reported that April had been a record month, with net earnings after taxes (but before depletion and depreciation) of $790,000. This was equal to an annual rate of $14 per share on capital stock. For the quarter ending on March 31, 44 new wells had been added, and some 20 new properties had been discovered and proven. Further, it was announced that a new casing head gasoline plant on the Burbank properties was nearing completion and would be operational by July 1. By then, it was estimated that the company would be producing more than 50,000 gallons of commercial gasoline daily at its five plants. Little wonder that in October L. E. was being listed as one of the "Men Who Make the Oil Industry."[18]

Throughout 1922 stories announced new and almost unbelievable successes on the Burbank leases, and that many recently drilled wells were flowing naturally at 1200 barrels per day. In September the company "started another drilling boom" in Butler County, Kansas, about 30 miles northwest of El Dorado.[19] There seemed to be no end to the boom for the Phillips Petroleum Company and, because of it, the Phillips brothers began increasingly to show personal interest in the welfare of the employees who had helped them realize such growth.

For some time, a stock option plan which permitted workers to buy into the company had been available. Then an insurance program was added, giving each employee with four years service a maximum of $4000 of personal life coverage. By January 1, 1923, a bonus system had been initiated which awarded each person with three years service a bonus of $50; each with four, $100;

and each with five years or more, $150. Because there then were "approximately 1,400 men" on the payroll, the latter gesture potentially could have cost Phillips Petroleum upwards of $200,000. Later a retirement program would be added to assure life income for faithful employees.[20]

Frank and L. E. were progressive administrators as well as tough-minded businessmen. They were almost universally respected as the brilliant co-founders of an important petroleum corporation.[21] L. E. also continued to be regarded as an outstanding banker as well as a prominent oilman, despite the fact that he had long since removed himself from active leadership in the bank. Once when a passerby saw him standing in front of the old Bartlesville National Bank Building, staring comtemplatively at the window, L. E. was asked, "Want to get back in there?" "No," Phillips replied, "but those were happy days." Such allusions grew less frequent, for L. E. truly was marking cobblestones in the petroleum industry. He was regarded as a financial expert, as one account read, "one of the men responsible for the up-building of the Phillips Petroleum Company, and one of the best informed oilmen in the Mid-Continent field." His responsibilities for the "credit and payments for his company" had given it an enviable, commanding position in the industry.[22]

With such growth, the question inevitably arose as to why the Phillips corporate headquarters and administrative staff were not moved to New York or to some other financial center, and some consideration actually was given to the idea. "I don't mind telling you," L. E. was quoted as saying, "that there was a time a short while ago . . . when the Phillips Petroleum Company seriously considered . . . removal from Bartlesville. The reason we decided to stay was because an investigation showed it had the best moral atmosphere of any town in the Southwest." He concluded: "We are here to stay."[23]

Phillips Petroleum chose to make Bartlesville its headquarters.
This building, built in two stages, was the first permanent office
complex constructed by P.P.C.

And so they were. They did not turn their backs completely on Gotham, but in 1925 they began the construction of a modern seven-story office building in Bartlesville while maintaining only a modest "base of operations" in New York. For too long, Bartlesville was and had been home for the Phillips brothers; they felt more comfortable among Western folk. Besides, railroads, airplanes, telephones, and telegraphs bridged the miles between Oklahoma and New York City for all but the most critical needs of the company. Neither Frank nor L. E. ever complained about the time spent or the inconvenience suffered in making long train trips to their Eastern office.

Some also marveled at their ability to attract and retain quality personnel in Bartlesville when other corporations located in cultural centers in the East seemed to offer so much more. Perhaps the Eastern attractions were not so enticing to Western-bred men, or perhaps Phillips knew what the interests of those men were. From the earliest times, the company provided a well-rounded recreation program with ever-expanding facilities. A basketball program, begun in 1920, grew to national prominence in later years and attracted an exceptionally talented group of college-educated athletes, many of whom rose to high administrative positions in Phillips Petroleum. Most notable, of course, was K.S., "Boots" Adams, who succeeded Frank Phillips as President upon his retirement. These men, like L. E. and Frank, enjoyed a simpler lifestyle, and they preferred the smaller city's environment as a general work setting. "They were," Philip R. Phillips once remarked about L. E. and Frank, "big fish in a little pond. The only thing was that the pond kept getting bigger."[24]

Indeed so. But if the pond was growing, the catalyst for much of the change was Phillips Petroleum. Almost from the beginning, Frank and L. E. were innovators. As early as 1917 they were concerned about the "waste" of enormous amounts of natural gas which most drillers allowed to escape into the atmosphere or burned by flame. This gas, which filled the air with a nauseous aroma, was regarded as worthless and of little more than nuisance value. The Phillips brothers were convinced otherwise. By October of 1917, they had constructed between Bartlesville and Dewey the Hamilton Gasoline Plant, the first plant "to extract liquids from natural gas."

With a battery of "newly hired engineers and scientists," they successfully developed a way to make marketable products out of natural gas. In 1923, Phillips established a separate Gas Sales Department to promote the sale of this product.[25]

With this success, Phillips set out further to produce, develop, and market the new product. By 1924 the company was the largest producer of natural gas liquids; by 1925 Phillips' scientists, now formally organized into a new research division, further refined the techniques of controlling the volatile elements in the product, and established a pilot plant near Shidler, Oklahoma, to develop uses for the byproducts which were removed by the so-called fractionation process. The Phillips brothers were not known for doing things halfway; they saw the vast potential of the expanding technology, and they were determined to lead the industry in it. L. E. fully believed that the next American business frontier would be in the field of chemistry. Not even a lawsuit, lodged by the Carbide and Carbon Chemical Corporation, which unsuccessfully claimed patent infringements on a similar process developed independently of Phillips' laboratories, slowed for long the research and development of Philgas, as the chief product was named.[26]

Philgas, a liquid petroleum gas, was a genuine success. With a companion development of manufacturing low-pressurized tanks, which the company made available to individual customers, the product was easy to market in areas not serviced by public utilities, particularly farm and rural communities. Paul Endacott, a principal in patenting these small pressurized tanks and later President of Phillips Petroleum Company, remembers well his assignment as regional sales manager for the Detroit area and the rapid acceptance of Philgas by Michiganders.[27]

With decisions made so wisely, both in the expansion of crude production and in pioneering new products,

Phillips Petroleum Company Directors inspecting the Burbank Field on April 4, 1923.

Frank and Lee Eldas built a financially solid corporation. From 1923 on, headlines chronicled their growth. "Phillips Company Makes Sensational Gain," was the headline on April 23, 1923, in the *Bartlesville Morning Examiner.* Quarterly earnings for the period ending March 31 were announced as $4,414,924, or the equivalent of $25 per share of outstanding stock on an annual basis, three times the earnings for the previous period in 1922. There were 1202 producing wells of record and a score of others in some stage of drilling. On the strength of that report, the stockholders of the company authorized a 100 percent increase in the number of outstanding shares of common stock in order to finance even greater expansion.[28]

Growing concern mounted again in mid-1923 over the effect of massive new oil production in California. Much pressure was being felt by petroleum companies in the Midwest, a region referred to in oil circles as the Mid-Continent fields. L. E. was vitally concerned with the problem, and he and others carefully analyzed a speech by E. W. Marland to the Western Petroleum Refiners in Kansas City on July 31, 1923. "A flood of low cost California oil" was having a menacing effect on the markets previously enjoyed by Oklahoma and Kansas producers. Many Mid-Continent companies had bulging storage tanks and declining sales but refused to lower their prices to customers already under firm contract. To combat the dilemma, Marland called for a suspension of refining for one month to help the industry adjust to what he believed would be only a temporary condition. By doing so, he said, the law of supply and demand would be whetted by planned shortages.[29]

Marland's remarks were but one response to a threat issued by L. V. Nicholas, president of the National Petroleum Marketers Association, that he would request a federal investigation if Mid-Continent oil prices were not lowered to 80 cents per barrel, then the market value of crude. Nicholas made his threat after petroleum producers began to prorate their oil shipments to pipeline companies, leaving Nicholas and the National Oil Marketers with insufficient volume to meet domestic and world demands.[30] His threat drew a flood of protests from Mid-Continent oilmen.

One of those protesting was L. E. Phillips. Nicholas, he declared publicly, was "an incomparable nut" who was behaving like a "parlor bolshevik." He praised his colleagues for their constructive and sensible actions, stating, "We cannot leave the industry to radicals with no monetary investment in the business, to come in and do things that would bring about stagnation and irreparable loss." To reduce the price to Nicholas' requested level would result in wells having to be plugged, because owners would lose money on oil produced and sold at

80 cents per barrel. Lee put Phillips Petroleum solidly behind the movement to rebuke and rebuff Nicholas.[31]

Withholding oil from the market hurt some oilmen who were dependent upon rapid sale of their production. Their dilemma encouraged large investors to explore the possibility of purchasing a controlling interest in beleaguered companies. Such men as Henry Ford and Pierre Samuel DuPont even had their representatives approach Phillips Petroleum and Skelly Oil companies "to test the waters." Waite Phillips received a bid of $55 million for his properties from the Roxana Petroleum Company. Skelly did make arrangements with Standard Oil of New Jersey during that year to dispose of "a large proportion" of the output of its refineries, but not its corporate stock.[31]

Phillips apparently gave scant consideration to these offers, and boldly responded by entering the money market at the turn of the year, offering 236,000 shares of treasury stock for sale at $30 a share. Frank and L. E. negotiated the sale in New York in order "to raise approximately $9 million so that the Phillips Company can actively bid for Osage oil and gas leases scheduled for auction the last of March.[33]

The new funding, according to L. E., was essential since "every oil company is under-financed," and all oil firms, big or small, needed more cash to seek new oil pools. "Despite persistent belief of the public that the oil industry is rich," he concluded, "some of the largest companies in the Mid-Continent field are starving for financial aid." He indicated that the public should be willing to supply some of the needed funds through increased prices at the pump; otherwise the alternative might be subsidization of the oil industry by government.[34]

For the Phillips Company, it was full speed ahead as 1924 began. Oil production was at its highest in company history. New wells in the Burbank field and in the Texas Panhandle, new gasoline plants which were designed to

use the newest oil absorption process, and two portable
charcoal plants in the Panhandle fields sparked new
optimism. Production ran so high that a large portion
of it had to be stored, and L. E. was obliged to announce
a new company policy, voluntarily imposed, which cut
drilling to a minimum by delaying all wildcatting on the
company's numerous leasehold blocks. In October,
Frank and L. E. announced that the company was negotiating for the purchase of the Indian Refining Company of Lawrenceville, Illinois. For the first time,
consideration was being shown toward expanding into
the refining end of the business.[35] Two years would pass,
however, before Phillips actually would refine any of the
crude it produced.

The financial report for the year ending December
31, 1924, was almost unbelievable. In only its seventh
year of existence, the Phillips Petroleum Company
showed assets of $103,407,043. There were 1456 pro-
ducing wells; oil production of 9,355,798 net barrels;
and 21 plants in operation with an output of 62,501,127
net gallons. It was increasingly obvious, not only to
Frank and L. E., but to the stockholders and directors
as well, that Phillips Petroleum had passed beyond the
wildcatting stage where individual wells were the primary focus. Indeed, with almost 1500 producing wells
and nearly a score of drilling rigs active on company
leases, and with a drilling record for the past year of
almost 90 percent success for every hole begun, the directors and administrators were forced to consider only
the larger picture of what it would take to keep their
growing giant virulent.[36]

Thus the Phillips brothers had begun their climb in
an industry which had no standards, few models, and
still fewer precedents. They were pioneering a new venture, in a learn-as-you-go environment. Why they survived when countless others failed is not an unexplained
miracle; rather it was the result of an entrepreneurial

spirit tempered by intelligence and planning. They stood toe-to-toe with the big oil interests of the East, surpassing most, and they fought the others to a standstill of mutual respect. The events of the next few years would project Phillips Petroleum to new heights in the industry, but there were more lessons to be learned and new innovations to be implemented before the company could be designated one of the leaders in the oil business.

6

PHILLIPS PETROLEUM COMES OF AGE

For L. E. and Frank, seven years of experience in a tough, boom-and-bust industry had taught them valuable lessons. Discoveries of new pools almost always were accompanied by periods of oversupply which drove prices below the costs of production. To survive these times required the storage of surpluses until demand approximated production, thus assuring a survival price and, hopefully, a profit for crude oil. Those companies which did not have storage capacity and which were dependent on sales at the time of production often found they could not endure a recession and were obliged to sell to or be absorbed by larger or more diversified companies. The appearance of the representatives of Henry Ford and Pierre DuPont in Oklahoma during the crisis resulting from the California oil glut came as no surprise to experienced oilmen. Their presence did not frighten L. E. or Frank.

Large financiers were notorious for their dealings with fledgling oil companies. Like sharks in a pool of small fish, they stayed around the edge until one of the smaller wildcatting firms got into financial difficulty, then would charge in for the kill, buying out its production and operation at depressed costs. The trick to survival, of course, was not to get caught in such a financial bind, yet to avoid this pitfall required careful planning and prudent financing. In both areas the Phillips brothers excelled. Early on, they built storage tanks to hold their surpluses; they developed new uses for their product to lessen their dependence on the sale of crude; they bought and built refineries to broaden their competitive edge in the industry; and by 1925 they had formed a division of sales and marketing which marked yet another cobblestone on their road to a full vertical integration of the company, from production and distribution to refining and retail sales of oil and its many byproducts. It was for that principal reason that Phillips Petroleum endured when countless others failed.

If 1924 represented a banner year, 1925 was even more dramatic; in fact, it was a sort of "coming out year," one in which the company took stock of itself and immensely liked what it saw on the accounting sheets. Corporate statistics almost always seem cold to disinterested readers, but L. E., once the firm's bookkeeper and auditor, must have felt nothing but sheer delight when he reflected about the figures. He could remember the early days when the company had assets of approximately $3 million; now they exceeded $130 million. The annual report which he reviewed for the year ending December 31, 1925, detailed a six-year growth in oil production, from less than 2 million barrels in 1920 to almost 10 million in 1925; in gasoline production, from 2-½ million gallons to almost 120 million gallons; in dividends paid, from zero to $4.6 million; and in net income, from $6.2 million to $21.2 million. "The aggregate worth today," a newsman summarized, "fairly entitles the Phillips Petroleum Company to be classified as one of the 'major' companies of the industry."[1] Indeed so!

Increasing pride characterized the firm after 1925. For several years it had been the practice of the company to invite the directors and several large stockholders to come to Bartlesville for the annual meeting. At first, these groups were small, and a simple inspection tour of nearby oil fields was arranged to acquaint them with "their" company and its holdings. By 1925, a tour of

Phillips holdings was a major undertaking. Undaunted and "busting with pride," Frank and L. E. planned an early modern safari-extravaganza for some 70 directors and major stockholders.

They had them meet on April 15 at Grand Central Station in New York City, most of them virtual strangers, to begin a trip by special train, "complete in every detail and convenience known to railroad service and equipment," which took them on a week-long tour of much of Phillips' vast oil empire. It was one of the most important gestures the Phillips brothers could have made, for the several days of close camaraderie welded the group into a family mold. So carefully was the trip planned by Charles R. Musgrave, Vice President for the Transportation Department, that all soon discovered that their thoughts needed to be only for one another. "But what else could be expected," a journalist recorded, "of hosts like Frank and L. E. Phillips, president and vice president . . . of one of the most efficient organizations in the oil industry?"[2]

The tour included stops in Fort Worth, Cisco, and Breckenridge, Texas, as well as all of the principal Oklahoma towns where Phillips operated oil fields and plants. The party was hailed at every stop by townspeople and the press, and they were feted with food and fun at major overnight stops. The accolades thrust upon the Phillips brothers were almost overwhelming, and the expanded knowledge of the oil industry gained by stockholders was profound. Word spread throughout the industry that Phillips Petroleum cared about its stockholders, that it indeed was a giant corporation and deserved the growing recognition it was receiving as a leader in the petroleum world.[3]

Following this grand tour, it was back to business as usual for L. E. and Frank, hard as it was to return to routine. Reflectively, L. E. observed, "At no time in the past ten years . . . has there been a condition like that at present, where there is no new oil pool in sight." He added that most of the older pools were declining, and that much of the new production was coming from deeper drilling. He made these gloomy observations to the press while he was in Boston to enroll Martha Jane in the Erskine School.[4] But Phillips Petroleum was expanding nonetheless. In November, Frank and L. E. announced a hike in the quarterly dividend rate to 75 cents; simultaneously they told of a new issue of 481,416 shares of capital stock which would be sold through Blair and Company of New York. In making this announcement, they pledged immediate and aggressive expansion, as well as completion of the building which they planned to use for corporate offices in Bartlesville. They expected to raise approximately $20 million from the sale of stock.[5]

The new stock issue and announced program of expansion coincided with the development of a new oil district in the Texas Panhandle, where Phillips recently had purchased a casing head gasoline plant. In December of 1925, Lee Eldas and other company officials made an inspection tour of the field 30 miles northeast of Amarillo and began negotiating for additional plant sites. Already the world's leader in production of casing head gasoline, Phillips was determined to retain that distinction.[6]

By April 18, 1926, when the stockholders again were in Bartlesville for their annual meeting, Phillips officials were able to announce that the company was the largest producer in the Panhandle, then acclaimed by oilmen as "the greatest potential oil field in the world." Phillips, they reported, was "sitting on top of the world" there, not only in oil production but also in the refining of natural gasoline. The stockholders again had been brought by special train from New York City to Bartlesville, but their itinerary included oil field visits only to nearby Oklahoma holdings.[7]

Shortly after the stockholders' meeting, L. E. decided
to vacation with his family in Hawaii, and while awaiting
passage on the steamship *Maui* in San Francisco, he was
interviewed by the *San Francisco Chronicle*. Always the
optimist, he stated that Phillips production again would
rise and that earnings might reach $12 per share of
outstanding stock in 1926. The company, he said, had
a total of 1998 producing wells, up from 1750 at the
same time in 1925, of which 21 were in the new Panhandle field. Demand for crude was high, and storage
supplies were diminishing daily due to a favorable price
structure.[8]

Upon his return in late August, he again was "inter-
cepted" by the *Chronicle*, and in an "hour's chat" with a
reporter reflected a "bullish outlook on the oil situation
in general." Lee regarded the industry as a "railroad or
public utility in its infancy" and believed that in time the
public would come to regard the securities of leading
companies as prime investments. Why, he was asked,
had Phillips enjoyed such phenomenal success? Because,
L. E. responded, its employees are among the most loyal
in the nation, and its executives are available 24 hours
a day. "Hard work and loyalty and use of common sense
have put Phillips in the strategic position that it
maintains."[9]

That "strategic position" was reflected in the annual
report for 1926. In an "almost incredible story of progress, expansion, and prosperity," Frank Phillips presented facts to the stockholders in Bartlesville that were
staggering: company assets were placed at $166,274,-
927; net earnings at $35,040,965; producing wells at
2293; and gross production at 20,083,266 barrels. In
addition to the financial statement, the stockholders
were given an appraisal of the future of the oil industry.
Despite frequent periods of overproduction, the industry had stabilized, due in large measure to increasing
demands for automobile gasoline. In 1910 there were

but 468,000 cars and trucks; by 1920 there were 8,-232,000; and by December 31, 1926, the number had risen to more than 22 million. The number would rise even higher in the future, and demand for gasoline would increase proportionally. Phillips, the report concluded, along with the industry in general, would supply whatever demands were placed on American oilmen. And, as if Phillips were preparing for the prophesied increased demand, the company announced the sale of $40 million in 5-½ percent bonds.[10] A check in the amount of $38,575,833.33, drawn by the firm of Harris, Forbes and Company, New York, was delivered to the Phillips Company on June 14, 1927, less than a month after the offer to sell was recorded—a true testimonial to investors' acceptance of Phillips' status and stability in the business world. L. E.'s earlier prediction about the value of oil company securities had been proven.[11]

An important factor in seeking new capital had been to secure funds for the purchase of Oklahoma's largest gas company, the Oklahoma Natural Gas Corporation, headquartered in Tulsa. Financial troubles had plagued the firm in recent months, and it had been taken over by a New York banking firm. Still, gas shortages and "unskilled administration" made many patrons in a service area of 50 cities in south-central Oklahoma unsatisfied and angry. Although this purchase caught many Tulsans by surprise, it was generally lauded in the press because it returned the company to Oklahoma ownership.[12] One light-hearted editorial indicated that all the "cussing" directed at the gas company could now be leveled at Frank Phillips. "In fact," the editor stated, "this writer has heard [Mr. Phillips] indulge in no little of that cussing himself. For in the old days he shivered for lack of gas, along with the plebian, and a shivering plute suffers quite as much as a shivering plebe."[13]

L. E. made the announcement of the purchase. In reassuring language, he stated that there would be no policy changes and no changes in management except that Phillips' directors would constitute the majority of the board with Frank Phillips as chairman. The firm would keep its headquarters in Tulsa. "It is the intention," L. E. stated, "to connect the present system with the Amarillo, Texas, field by laying over 200 miles of 22-inch pipe, which will insure to Oklahoma a more stable and permanent supply of gas for the future." He concluded, "It is anticipated that the purchase of the Oklahoma Natural will eventually give Phillips a larger outlet for its natural gas."[14]

Interestingly, only a few months separated the purchase from another dramatic announcement: the sale of Oklahoma Natural Gas to the American Natural Gas Corporation for approximately $40 million, a sum which represented "a fair profit" for Phillips over its rumored purchase price of $25 million. In confirming the sale, Frank Phillips stated that the reason for the original acquisition was to secure an additional market for his company's large production of natural gas. Not only was this assurance validated by the contract of sale, but also the intent to build the proposed pipeline from the Amarillo fields was reconfirmed.[15]

As fate would have it, a mild recession again confronted the Mid-Continent producers at this time because of a surfeit of oil produced in the revived Greater Seminole Field. Active over a number of years, the Seminole Field began declining during late 1925, causing many oilmen to abandon it. Then, in rapid succession, three new pools boomed into production in the spring of 1926, flooding the market with excess crude. Phillips added new wells there during the 18-month-long boom and felt the pressure of oversupply along with other producers. There was a clamor throughout the Mid-Continent area for curtailment of production.[16]

Interviewed in Wichita, where he had gone to deliver an address to the Chamber of Commerce, L. E. re-

*The development of a new aviation fuel, lighter and more pow-
erful than regular commercial gasoline, paved the way for victory in the Dole Derby and in the marketing of Phillips 66
gasoline in company-owned service stations after 1928.*

sponded to the usual queries about shutting down production until Seminole surpluses were absorbed. He
stated that the oil industry was driven by land purchases
which require drilling within a specified period of time.
These contracts could not be abrogated without severe
penalties; thus once committed, the drilling must take
place despite industry-wide production conditions. That
was why, he explained, that Seminole crude was having
such a sharp impact on the price of oil. Only time and
a predicted drop in Seminole production would adjust
marketing conditions. Despite his opinion and a host of
supporting protests, a successful plea by the Gypsy Oil
Company for a restraining order was honored by the
Oklahoma Corporation Commission, a body which was
empowered by law to arbitrate cases involving wastage
of petroleum resources. Although Phillips Petroleum

L.E. Phillips congratulates Art Goebbel, pilot of the Woolaroc, *who won the $25,000 Dole Derby first prize by flying non-stop, San Francisco to Honolulu, in August, 1927.*

was not a big Seminole Field producer, L. E. joined his protesting colleagues, but to no avail. The injunction stood, and operators were constrained from further drilling in certain parts of the Seminole Field. The controversy eventually led to the proration of well production in Oklahoma, an action later expanded into federal regulations. The Greater Seminole Field, as it was called, was the last in Oklahoma where wells were allowed to produce at full capacity.[17]

Another triumph for Phillips scientists occurred in 1927. After several years of research and countless hours of testing, an improved aviation fuel was developed which was named "New Aviation Natural." Many pilots and plane manufacturers had collaborated in the experiment, and the fuel had been tested in at least one coast-to-coast flight. The new fuel, which was made from casing head gasoline by a special process, weighed a half pound less per gallon than regular gasoline and delivered much greater power.[18] To test the new gasoline properly under actual conditions, Frank decided, with L. E.'s full support, to sponsor a plane in the Dole Air Race, a competitive flight from Oakland, California, to Hawaii with a winner's purse of $25,000. James D. Dole, Hawaii's pineapple king, had offered the prize to the first pilot to fly non-stop to Wheeler Field in Honolulu starting at noon, Pacific Time, August 12, 1927.

Frank first made arrangements through Fred Capshaw, chairman of the Corporation Commission in Oklahoma City, to join in supporting the airplane of Bennett H. Griffin, then in its final stages of construction at Wichita, Kansas. Known as the *Oklahoma*, the craft was a Travel Air monoplane and was powered by a Wright Whirlwind engine, identical to the one which powered Lindberg's *Spirit of St. Louis*. Later Frank became interested in a second plane when its pilot, Hollywood stunt flyer Arthur C. Goebel, approached him with a desperate plea for financial assistance. Impressed, Frank advanced Goebel $3500, the amount needed to complete the payment for a Travel Air identical to Griffin's. The craft would become known as *Woolaroc*, in honor of Frank's famous ranch.[19]

The two entries brought Phillips some enviable publicity "which couldn't be purchased at any price, for it's been front page stuff everywhere and will be front page stuff for some time to come." And the attention given to the new aviation fuel, which both airships would use exclusively, was music to Phillips' ears. Frank was convinced that the world was "in the vestibule of a new era of transportation," and it made good business sense to be in the forefront of the development of aviation fuel.[20]

Both flyers began their missions from Bartlesville, arriving at the Municipal Airport at Oakland, California, a few days before the official start of the "Dole Derby." Both took off on August 16, 1927, for their Hawaii rendezvous. Griffin had drawn the right to be first in taking off, but unfortunately he lost this advantage a few minutes after he became airborne. His engine developed mechanical trouble when the ninth cylinder "froze," and he was forced to withdraw from the competition. Goebel, who had drawn the seventh position, "hopped off from the mainland" at 12:36 p.m. P.S.T., and after a continuous flight of 26 hours, 17 minutes, and 20 seconds, landed the *Woolaroc* at Wheeler Field on Oahu at 12:33 p.m. Honolulu time. Goebel, aided by his navigator, Navy Lieutenant W. C. Davis, arrived first by almost two hours! "Honest to gosh," a disbelieving Goebel asked upon landing, "do you mean that I am really the first one here?"[21]

The triumph was tumultous! Because of the increasing public interest in distance flying which Lindbergh's trans-Atlantic flight had generated, newspapers everywhere hailed Goebel's feat. He was an instant hero, although a nonstop flight from the mainland to the islands had been accomplished twice previously. Frank beamed over the victory. "We have tremendous faith," he said, "in the future of aviation. It is because of a desire to do our part in its progress that the Phillips' organization has been working so diligently on the airplane fuel problem." L. E. was playfully ecstatic. Now that a Phillips' plane had won the race, L. E. wired Dole, a personal friend, that he was sending "a couple of boys over" to collect the money. With some profundity he concluded to Dole, "Goebel's indomitable courage, Dole's pineapple money, and Phillips' gas turned the trick. Turn over the money."[22] However, the long celebration which followed was marred by the fact that two airships and crews were lost at sea during the race.

The following year, Phillips expanded its interests in the field of aviation by organizing a new company to begin the manufacture of airplanes. Though a separate entity, a Phillips Vice President, John H. Kane, was

Tenth Annual Meeting of the Directors of Phillips Petroleum, April 19, 1927.

named President, and Frank and L. E., among others, were named to the board of directors. The plane, "a light, two seater, highwing, cabin monoplane," was equipped with a 70-horsepower engine capable of achieving a maximum of 105 miles per hour. Fitted with limousine-style upholstery, it was designed for the convenience and comfort of businessmen and sportsmen. Production was not long lived; Phillips shortly thereafter discontinued making the Cavalier, as it was named.[23]

If 1925 was the "coming out year" for Phillips, 1927 was the year of total vertical integration of the growing giant. Long priding itself in being only in the production end of the oil game, Phillips was forced by industry pressures to move into other phases of the petroleum business. Building storage tanks to help soften the impact of periodic oil gluts which sent prices spiraling downward had helped stabilize Phillips position during the dirst decade. By 1925, however, the larger inde-

PANTEX CAMP LOOKING NORTH

A part of Phillips Pantex Field near Borger in the Texas Panhandle.

pendents as well as the major national oil corporations had built their own storage facilities, especially firms such as Standard Oil of Indiana, which was heavily into the refining and retailing of gasoline. Increasingly, such companies provided their own production, which put enormous pressure on oil firms such as Phillips which were engaged primarily in supplying crude and other basic oil products.

Moreover, the tests which produced the new aviation fuel had brought under Phillips' exclusive control a product which was vastly superior to contemporary ordinary motor fuel. Yet to move into the highly competitive fields of refining and retail distribution was gutty— a truly momentous decision. "The future of the company depended in no small measure upon the success of this gigantic undertaking."[24]

Movement came with lightning speed. In October, Phillips announced its intention to build a giant refinery in the Texas Panhandle near Borger, site of a rapidly developing field in which Phillips already had a commanding position.[25] Then, to complete the cycle, what was then regarded as a "small scale" experiment to test public acceptance of a new gasoline, called Phillips 66, was begun with the construction of four stations. Phillips

Phillips Petroleum opened its first retail service station on Central Avenue in Wichita, Kansas, in November, 1927. Others followed in a rapid expansion which produced nearly 600 retail outlets in an 18-month span.

66 gasoline was first sold in Wichita, Kansas, on November 19, 1927; a week later, a second test station opened in Salina, Kansas. The third and fourth soon followed in Topeka, Kansas, and Bartlesville, Oklahoma. Public acceptance was instantaneous. News spread about its high volatility, quick ignition, and rapid acceleration features. By May of 1928, sales had exceeded all expectations, and the task then was to build a complete organization to market the product. "Never in the history of the oil industry," a company report summarized, "was a complete system of sales outlets established with greater speed."[26] Purchase and construction of retail and bulk (supply and storage) stations in neighboring states were undertaken rapidly, and bulk stations for a time were established at the rate of one per day. And Boeing Air Transport exclusively adopted the new aviation "high compression" gasoline for its mail service between Chicago, Omaha, and Salt Lake City.[27] In a short span

Executive Committee Meeting, for which L.E. Phillips served as Chairman from 1929 to 1933. L to R: John Kane, L.E., Clyde Alexander, Frank, Ray Hamilton, unidentified, W.N. Davis.

of time, Phillips achieved "a place among the leaders in sales in all states" in which it operated. As one account stated in early 1929, "The Phillips Petroleum Company is producer, refiner, marketer, and exporter of oil and oil products. It has forty-nine gasoline plants and refineries and owns a fleet of 2,122 tank cars."[28] L. E. and Frank in 12 years had moved from a single-purpose structure operated by two brothers and 27 employees to a full-service operation managed by a giant corporate structure and large administrative staff. The two brothers were still in command, but their roles were changing dramatically.

Frank more and more was in New York, although he spent much time in Bartlesville, in his presidential functions. But recognizing that a corporate management team required greater supervision of its Vice Presidents and division heads, to whom segments of responsibility were delegated, the board of directors at its 1929 annual meeting "retired" L. E. from his role as Vice President and General Manager and elected him the first chairman of the Executive Committee. Clyde Alexander was elected to L. E.'s old position.[29]

Growth personified the surging Phillips Company in the early months of 1929. First quarter earnings were placed at $3,612,879, as compared to $3,105,091 for the corresponding period of the previous year. Several new wells were completed in Hutchinson County, Texas, and in Butler, Ellis, and Greenwood counties in Kansas. Three new natural gas plants were begun in the Panhandle oil fields. And L. E. confirmed a report that Phillips was joining three other oil firms, the Texas Company, Skelly Oil Company, and Columbia Carbon Company, in developing plans for constructing a pipeline to Chicago from the Texas Panhandle. But it was in the accounts of the earnings report for the third quarter that a high note was truly sounded. The "ho-hum, we did it again," analysis of earnings showed $6,518,518 for 1929 as compared to $5,846,156 for 1928. It was in retail marketing where the true drama unfolded. Phillips now was operating nearly 600 retail stations; annual sales were running at approximately 100 million gallons (as compared to 10 million gallons the previous year!); and the company had developed and was marketing a higher octane gasoline, which it called Phillips 66 Ethyl—all in the span of less than two years.[30]

There were ominous clouds hanging over the business world in mid-October, 1929. A sudden selling spree sent stock market prices plummeting. They recovered briefly, but the end was far from over. Frank, whose job it was to work with the New York financial community, received assurances from his most trusted contacts that "the bottom has undoubtedly been reached" and that "a full recovery could be anticipated." Accepting their analysis, he reported that "underlying conditions are sound, leading exchanges have weathered the ordeal, and the situation will soon right itself."[31]

When a record 16 million shares were "dumped" on

the market on October 29, hysteria set in despite repeated assurances from Wall Street spokesmen that the
market had stabilized and would recover. It was at that
point that Frank showed the true mettle of Phillips Petroleum. Believing that the company owed something
to its stockholders, he called an emergency meeting of
the executives and explained that, although the Phillips'
stock still had solid value, the "little fellows outside do
not know that." If they joined the panic, he reasoned,
they one day might regret it. His proposal was that each
of the 6000 stockholders of record should have an immediate communication from the company which would
offer them encouragement. All agreed. Sixteen telegraph operators were imported hurriedly from Tulsa
and Wichita, and they worked from eight o'clock in the
evening until four o'clock the next morning at the task.
Do not sell, each stockholder was told; hold on, for the
value was still there. "Very human sort of rich men are
the Phillips brothers," a feature writer opined, heaping
praise on Frank and L. E. for caring about their stockholders. "There are many millionaires in this world
... [but] only a few of them who deserve to be. Frank
and L. E. Phillips we number among them."[32]

The depression had set in. Times ahead seemed precarious because no one knew the depths to which the
economy would fall. The Phillips brothers had a business
to run, and economic distress was nothing new to them.
Speaking on November 12, 1929, L. E. reminded the
public that in the oil business "there is usually feast or
famine." He declined any attempt to interpret the stock
market situation, concluding that the recent slump did
not mean that the earning power of good enterprises
had decreased. "It has not affected us in the least," he
said, "but I must say that I am proud of a country that
could withstand the tremendous shock of a $50 million
deflation without crashing. It speaks well for the stability
and sanity of the country."[33]

L.E. riding in an antique automobile while visiting a Phillips 66 station in Illinois.

L. E. set out almost immediately as a sort of personal emmisary to the operators of newly acquired service outlets. On November 6 he was in Des Moines meeting with local managers, supervisors, and salesmen in the Iowa division. When Phillips Petroleum bought 76 John Hancock service stations in the Twin Cities area, he went to Minneapolis in mid-December to help convert those operations to the Phillips system of merchandising. When he was not busy at that task, he was in places like Omaha negotiating for the right to furnish natural gas for that city's needs. There was no loss of intensity, but Lee Eldas did find time for a little diversion by attending the annual Gridiron Club Banquet in Washington, D.C. in December of 1929.[34]

What urged L. E. to embark on a world cruise at such a critical time in the nation's economy is unclear. Unquestionably it was a reflection of optimism for both country and company, but it may also have mirrored an increasing physical debilitation which was difficult for him to keep under control. After a short delay, occa-

L.E. at a station in Grand Rapids, Michigan.

sioned by an emergency appendectomy for son Philip Rex, L. E. and Node began their cruise on February 14, returning May 14, 1930. From the numerous telegrams L. E. received in connection with the voyage, it is obvious that friends and relatives alike hoped that the long respite would improve his health.[35]

While he was away, Phillips Petroleum was laying plans to construct a 1000-mile pipeline from "Borger, Texas, through Oklahoma and Kansas to Wichita, thence to Kansas City and on to St. Louis." A new company, the Phillips Pipeline Company, with Clyde Alexander as President, was formed to construct and operate the line. By June, surveys had been completed, pipe bought, and delivery was imminent. A completion date of January 1, 1931, was projected. The enormous undertaking bore a cost estimate of $15 million. Using a machine which dug two miles of ditch per day that was

Aerial view of present Bartlesville. Almost every major building shown in the center of this photograph is owned or leased by Phillips Petroleum, evidence of the immense economic importance of the company to Bartlesville.

40 inches deep and 18 inches wide, workers were able to lay 800 miles of eight-inch pipe in one year, completing the enormous task in August of 1931. Originally scheduled to open in January, the project was delayed when St. Louis county landowners, through legal action, sought to prevent the pipeline from crossing their property. A formal dedication hailed the completion of the line, and Frank turned the first spigot to allow gasoline to flow into the tank of a car driven by Mayor Frank Doyle of East St. Louis, in whose city the terminal station and refinery were located.[36]

Also in the summer of 1930, Bartlesville residents learned that a new expansion of corporate offices was soon to begin. Barely four years after the new office building had been opened, it was evident that additional space would be required to house the executives of an expanding major oil firm. Two floors were to be added to the relatively new headquarters building. Additionally, one eight-story wing and a ten-floor office tower were projected. And for good measure, it was announced that another floor would be added to the First National Bank building—all this in the thick of the nation's worst depression. It was another indelible expression of faith in the future by Phillips Petroleum.[37]

Later that summer, a news bombshell exploded, first in rumor form—which was confirmed on August 29, 1930. A merger had been arranged and approved by both boards of directors, uniting Phillips Petroleum with the Independent Oil and Gas Company of Tulsa, a firm headed by Waite Phillips, younger brother of L. E. and Frank.[38] The consolidation was big news. "The largest independent oil company in the world was created yesterday," one newspaper recorded, "when the three famous Phillips brothers of Tulsa and Bartlesville decided to consolidate their holdings." Another paper styled it "a truce in the battle of brothers over oil development in the Mid-Continent area." Still another headlined, "Brothers Unite Under One Business Flag Again." News coverage was widespread, and the stories of how the three brothers had achieved their lofty goals were recounted almost to the point of vainglory.[39]

Waite had left his brothers in 1914. He went to Fayetteville, Arkansas, opened a chain of filling stations, and entered the wholesale gasoline business. In 1916, he moved to Okmulgee, bought an oil lease near a graveyard, and later sold it to the Atlantic Petroleum Company for $200,000. He then moved to Tulsa in 1919. In 1920 he became a refiner with a plant at Okmulgee, and in 1922 organized the Waite Phillips Company with extensive holdings, both in oil and refining, in Oklahoma and Kansas. By 1925 his company was valued at $30 million, and in October of that year, he sold it to Blair and Company of New York, who subsequently resold it to the Barnsdall Oil Company in January of 1926.[40]

The sale made Waite independently wealthy, and he retired temporarily from the petroleum business. But idleness irked him and he soon returned to the oil business, scoring sensational successes. In 1927 he merged his new venture, the Philmack Company, with the Independent Oil and Gas Company of Tulsa. Waite became chairman of the board of the new firm, was its largest stockholder, and allowed the name of the consolidated companies to continue as the Independent Oil and Gas Company.[41]

The agreement between the Phillips Company and the Independent ended a "chain of rumors" which had circulated for some time that the brothers would reunite. The simple fact that L. E. and Frank would not leave Bartlesville and that Waite wanted to stay in Tulsa held off the consolidation for several months. Then during a retreat at Philmont, Waite's beautiful New Mexico ranch, in the summer of 1930, the "getting together" took place following lengthy discussions about maintaining two separate offices and current operations officers in Bartlesville and Tulsa.[42]

The merger exposed some impressive figures. Phillips had 3,378,822 shares of outstanding stock valued at $37.34 per share; the Independent had 1,379,295 shares outstanding with a $28.92 evaluation per share, and an exchange rate of roughly 76 shares of Phillips stock for each 100 shares of Independent stock was agreed upon. The combined assets approximated $316 million, of which more than $103 million was charged to reserves of all kinds, with net cash and current assets of more than $40 million. As of July 31, 1930, Phillips showed a balance sheet of net paid up capital of $126,145,173 of which $36,777,628 represented earned surplus. The Independent, the same date, reported net paid up capital of $39,622,836 of which $9,110,342 was earned surplus. The consolidation brought together a combined acreage of 2.6 million under leases in Oklahoma, Kansas, Texas, New Mexico, Arkansas, Colorado, Michigan, California, Louisiana, and Kentucky. Net production was almost 125,000 barrels a day from 3686 wells. There were 54 natural gas plants with a daily output of approximately one million gallons. The two merged companies had 1600 bulk and service stations, approximately 10,000 other affiliates and three refineries.[43]

The Phillips brothers, by their action, inscribed a large new cobblestone to mark their paths to a greatness that would become legendary. For the immediate future, the road was paved with pure savings at a time when economies of operation were growing more critical. "The physical properties of the two companies," a statement issued jointly by Phillips and the Independent read, "are of such character as to effect an immediate reduction in capital expenditures, and are located as to supplement each other without duplication, thus contributing to the natural economies of this consolidation amounting to several million dollars annually."[44]

Soon after the merger was consumated, L. E. became involved in discussions with Secretary of War Patrick J. Hurley, a long-time friend, and Major General Thomas Q. Ashburn, chairman of the federal Inland Waterways Corporation. Hurley had announced that almost $400 million would be spent in improving water passage on the Mississippi River and its tributaries, eventually connecting New Orleans with the Great Lakes and providing continuous access to St. Paul, Minnesota. Hurley had invited L. E. to join him and a party on an inspection tour of the River from St. Louis to New Orleans on September 9-16, 1930.[45]

While aboard Hurley's special riverboat, L. E. laid before General Ashburn a tentative plan for transporting crude oil or gasoline on river barges. Pipelines along the western banks of the Mississippi could transfer oil to the barges for shipment to places up and down the Mississippi River and its tributaries, and ultimately, through the port of New Orleans, to the Southeastern and Eastern states. Ashburn was impressed and even discussed the possibility of government-operated barges sponsored by the Inland Waterways Corporation. Secretary Hurley spoke enthusiastically about wanting to approve any plan which would "utilize the channels along the river to the fullest extent" and provide relief to the unemployed in river districts. By October, L. E.'s ideas had become Ashburn's plan, and he submitted a proposal to Phillips for inland water transportation which would complement the proposed construction of the oil line to St. Louis. Using that terminus as a loading point, barges, constructed either by the Inland Waterways Corporation by by oil producers themselves, would be filled with oil and towed to appropriate destinations. Discussions continued; the completion of the pipeline remained months into the future.[46]

The first full year of the depression for Phillips showed gains in gross income over 1929, and the company was able to declare a dividend greater than the company's stated minimums for the first three quarters. However, the general decline of stock values "carried the price of our stock to the lowest level in years," but management confidently predicted that those who held the stock would, if patient, ultimately be highly rewarded. The biggest problem facing the industry at year's end was overproduction. Phillips reported that daily production was being reduced by one-half the capacity of the previous year. Expansion in retail markets continued apace, nonetheless. Philip Rex Phillips, then district sales manager for the Springfield, Illinois, region, announced an aggressive construction and purchase plan for developing service stations in that new market area.[47]

L.E. learned from his heritage. This cave on the old Conway farm, which kept milk and meat cool, gave him the idea in the 1930s to store gasoline underground at Phillips service stations.

L. E. was anything but pessimistic. To speed economic recovery, he wrote his friend, Patrick Hurley, that the old slogan "See America first" should be revived and popularized. Vast sums of money spent annually on foreign tourism would go a long way toward relieving unemployment and reestablishing some degree or normalcy. "I feel sure," he said, "the weight of pessimism today centers around New York . . . . If the people there could get a breath of good fresh Oklahoma ozone or Colorado air, and see the cornfields of Iowa and the wheat fields of Kansas, that would do much to reestablish in the minds of many a more secure optimism." Secretary Hurley was so impressed that he laid L. E.'s proposal before the Department of Commerce and President Hoover's Unemployment Commission for further consideration.[48]

There was foundation for his optimism. In a report carried in the *Wall Street Journal* in May of 1931, L. E. was quoted as saying the company was in such a strong cash position that all sinking fund requirements for Phillips' bond issues were sufficient to pay in full all coupons due on June 1, 1931. "The company," he continued, "is experiencing the greatest volume of sales in history, and even with oil and products at present low levels, it is able to make an operating profit." "Phillips is," he concluded, "getting along perhaps as well as anyone in the industry," and the new Oklahoma City properties were proving to be some of the most valuable leases and would in the future provide sufficient revenues to retire all outstanding bonds.[49]

He spoke from proven facts. The Oklahoma City oil field, which embraced much of the land incorporated within the city itself, was indeed a fabulous find. Phillips, among countless others, rushed into action and met with instant success. On May 18, 1931, a well known as No. 1 McBeth was tested at an unbelievable rate of approximately 100,000 barrels a day, and some experts were prophesying that it might rank as the world's largest "sweet oil producer."[50]

The new, almost runaway production from this field, however, served only to heighten tensions within the industry. Overproduction along with depressed economic tensions already had driven prices of crude oil to a ridiculous record low of 22 cents a barrel. A meeting was called for July 10, 1931, in Oklahoma City, and virtually all operating and pipeline companies, as well as numerous royalty owners, met and discussed ways to combat the situation. The solution was obvious: stop production until demand approximated supply and prices adjusted accordingly. There was talk of renewed voluntary cooperation to limit production, but eventually a resolution was adopted by a vote of 73-3 which called for Governor W. H. Murray to close down production in the Oklahoma City pool until prices rose again to a dollar a barrel.[51]

A royalty owner, speaking in support of the resolution, said that if wells were shut down now, we "can lose only 22 cents a barrel, but if chaos continues . . . we may have to pay the pipeline companies to take our oil away." L. E. was more somber in his endorsement of the proposal. He urged caution and consistency in the policy being adopted, but lauded the fact that demoralization had, for the first time, forced both operators and royalty owners onto common ground for action. Once the resolution was ratified, it was forwarded to the Governor as well as to the Oklahoma Corporation Commission.[52]

On July 28, Governor Murray responded positively to the resolution. "The state and schools," the Governor said, "are getting nothing in the way of taxes from oil at the present price . . . . We can't let this go on depleting our resources and getting no taxes from them." With that statement he issued an ultimatum: raise the price of crude oil to a dollar a barrel by midnight Saturday, August 1, or face a forced shutdown of all production except for stripper wells. The impact of the decree was welcomed by independent oil producers, but the large purchasers of crude were incensed, most of whom thought the Governor had exceeded his authority. This was particularly true of Harry Sinclair, who made it known that he would continue to pay no more than the current top market price of 50 cents regardless of the Governor's edict. Other purchasers joined him, and their stubbornness cast a gloomy shadow over the impending showdown. The threat caused some upward movement in prices as the week waned, but the deadline passed without direct action. On August 4, Governor Murray ordered the National Guard into the oil fields, first closing five wells belonging to the Champlin Oil Company, which was already testing in federal court the proration ordered earlier by the Oklahoma Corporation Commission. The shutdown was extended to cover all of the 3106 wells in Oklahoma with a production of more than 25 barrels daily. Martial law reigned throughout the oil fields, while oil producers generally applauded the action.[53]

East Texas oil producers taunted the governor. That field also was experiencing large-scale overproduction, and producers there sent telegrams to "a number of refining companies" in Oklahoma offering to supply all their needs at 10 to 15 cents per barrel on the loading racks in East Texas. Such outrageous waste moved the Texas legislature into action, and on August 12, 1931, a bill was sent to Governor Ross Sterling which gave authority to the Railroad Commission to control oil production in Texas as a conservation measure. Sometime thereafter Governor Sterling used martial law to close the East Texas oil fields. Crude prices had dipped to a low of five to seven cents a barrel.[54]

In Oklahoma there were signs by August 12 that the deadlock between purchasers and the governor was weakening. After eight days of shutdown, at least one refinery, Cushing Refining and Gasoline Company, advised Governor Murray that it was in need of crude and would pay a dollar a barrel to obtain it from wells now closed. On August 24, Phillips also was to post prices at one dollar per barrel. Still there was no general movement upward until on August 19 the price reached 75 cents. Adamant almost to a fault, the governor remained steadfast, even when crude prices reached 85 cents in September. Oil purchasers maintained equal rigidity, and when Texas oil began to replace Oklahoma oil, Murray first relaxed the ban for 17 days and then removed it to allow production on a regular basis but with a regulation on total output from all wells in Oklahoma. Proration had begun in earnest and would remain a permanent feature of oil production in Oklahoma.[55]

Hardly had the dispute begun when a near-tragedy struck Phillips Petroleum. L. E. Phillips, at home for lunch on August 22, 1931, suddenly fainted, revived briefly, then became unconscious again, remaining in that condition from 1:00 p.m. until 9:15 p.m. For a time, his condition seemed very serious. Node, who was in Kansas City, promptly flew back to Bartlesville with daughter Martha Jane late in the evening. Finally, doctors were able to stabilize his condition and to diagnose his ailment as an attack of acute indigestion. He improved rapidly and was pronounced "out of danger" the following day. By August 28 he was reported to have a good appetite and was "up and around" the house. Frank expressed the opinion that L. E. would be back in his office within a few days.[56]

Lee Eldas did return to his office, but his work schedule was much reduced. The seriousness of his illness was to be measured by periodic absences rather than from his spoken, reassuring words. The rather obvious gap in scrapbook entries between August and November indicates an absence of business and social functions for the period. He did attend the annual meeting of the Anchor Club in Bedford, Iowa, in late October, and he made a special effort to hear the Phillips 66 Fliers, a company band, play a concert for radio broadcast on November 4.[57] He then hosted a family dinner in celebrating his and Node's wedding anniversary on the 26th, and had a funny story written about him on December 22 in a Bartlesville newspaper. Even that story may have made reference to his tender stomach:

> Did you know one of Bartlesville's richest and most influential men, a man who has been wined and dined on three continents and in the islands of the seas takes his greatest pleasure in eating cornmeal mush with nothing but skimmed milk on it. And he likes to eat in the kitchen.[58]

Others, later in his life, would witness him eating simple and easily digestible fare, even at civic functions, because of digestive deficiencies.[59]

After the turn of the year, his schedule increased. He attended and spoke to a divisional sales conference in Wichita and sounded like the L. E. of old. He declared the oil industry to be heading in the right direction, that it was in a strong position, and that it would play a leading role in the revival of business. In March he had a driving accident, striking a hawk in flight which penetrated his windshield, resulting in several scratches about his face. He was spared serious injury because he had turned his head slightly to speak with someone in the rear seat just before the impact. In April he was in Illinois and Indiana on business, but his name, once prominently mentioned in newspaper accounts of Phillips annual board meetings, was conspicuous by its absence.[60]

Perhaps one scrapbook entry mirrored L. E.'s waning interest in the push-and-shove of business activities, which had been so characteristic of his zest for the oil industry. A long article from a Nebraska newspaper, entitled "Romance Gone From the Oil Fields," referred to the new era of proration. Stabilization of production, the item summarized, was a boon to the industry, "but it eliminates the gambling that made men like the Phillips brothers from Iowa, millionaires almost overnight." The lure gone and health precarious, L. E. must have begun to think of retirement.[61]

In early September, L. E. returned to the Battle Creek Sanitarium in Michigan for a rest and a physical checkup. He had been a "guest" at the Sanitarium off and on for 22 years, his first visit having been in 1910. His present visit to the health institute at the Sanitarium was his first since 1926. Node also was an infrequent "guest," and she spent a part of the several weeks of his convalescence with him. Frank also flew there in his Ford Tri-Motor to check on his progress.[62]

Leaving the Sanitarium in improved health, L. E. motored through several states on his return to Bartlesville. He made short speeches in Minneapolis and Des Moines, always with optimism for the future and enthusiasm for the oil industry. And he paid his aging mother a brief visit in Conway on the last leg of his journey. Back at work, he joined other officials in boosting the company's semi-annual "Employees' Sales Drive," a marketing scheme which called on every Phillips' worker to sell Phillips products to neighbors, friends, or relatives. "The campaign," L. E. was quoted as saying, "is bound to be mutually beneficial . . . because an additional, large volume of business will expand the distribution of '66 products."[63]

Apparently, L. E. had camouflaged his trip to Battle Creek quite well. Few knew just how run down and weak he really was. But at Christmas time, an old stalwart friend, H. H. McClintock, in his annual letter to Lee Eldas, told him in cryptic language that he finally had realized the true state of his health. "Moses," McClintock wrote, "went up into the mountain" for there were no sanitariums in those days. "At last," he concluded, "all is clear and we have a deep appreciation for your days of travail," adding paranthetically for emphasis, "of which we were so grossly ignorant."[64]

Frank was not ignorant of his brother's growing hypertension and stomach disorders, nor were members of his family. They at first merely urged him to slow down, to accept a lesser work load, and to take more time away from Phillips Petroleum and Bartlesville. But the old workhorse instinct frequently "drove him back into harness." His speeches began to take on the flavor of the elder statesman, for he began to criticize federal regulations openly. "Oil," he said in Miami during a period of relaxation in the sunshine, "will be the first big business to show the way out of the depression, but it is so handicapped by taxation that so far recovery has been very difficult." Both he and Frank were convinced that the entire oil industry was carrying an inordinate burden in taxation.[65]

It is interesting to note that Frank joined L. E. in Florida for a brief respite from the cold weather of New York, perhaps out of brotherly concern. And it is informative to list the number of references throughout 1933 to L. E.'s need for rest. In Des Moines in June, his nurse broke up a brief reunion visit with four childhood friends and adamantly led him away to take his afternoon nap. He spent a few weeks in late summer in Colorado for rest and "the benefit of his health." And in October, while returning to Bartlesville from Cimarron, New Mexico, he was involved in an automobile accident which required hospitalization in Dodge City, Kansas. Though only slightly injured, he suffered more from nervousness, an overreaction to the trauma of overturning his car. He then spent a few days in Wichita at L. E., Jr.'s, home, and Philip Rex also came to check on his condition.[66]

Philip Rex Phillips, L. E.'s oldest son, recalls that it was becoming evident at this time that his father should retire completely, and all the family started to exert mild pressure on him to do so. A rather prolonged visit to the Thornton and Minor Clinic in Kansas City, a hospital he had frequented and relied upon for the treatment of his entire family, must have further weakened his resolve to "remain in harness" as a Phillips executive. The seriousness of his afflictions was reflected in the words of relief written by H. H. McClintock to L. E. while he was in Kansas City: "I want to tell you how happy I am over the good news I received from Nora last evening . . . . It's great to know that you are quite yourself again and can do the things in which you have so much pleasure."[67]

Christmas came joyfully at home. He gathered about himself his three children and their children. He now was a grandfather three times over, L. E., Jr., having two children and Martha Jane one. It was an excellent holiday season and a time for reflection. "I have been away from my office," he wrote a friend in Germany shortly after the new year began, "a great deal the last year, on account of sickness, but . . . am much improved in health; in fact, almost as good as new." "Almost" was not enough for his family, for Frank, or for Waite. This time their persistence bore fruit, and L. E. made his retirement official at the annual meeting of stockholders and directors in April of 1934.[68]

There were exciting years ahead for L. E., mostly fun-filled activities to which he could lend himself as health permitted or interest motivated. The respect which he had earned through the years as a banker, an oilman, and an unselfish civic worker kept him constantly in demand as a speaker or leader in various enterprises. And he continued to serve on the Kansas City Federal Reserve Bank Board, a truly prestigious appointment which he cherished and worked hard at. Although he was to sever his official ties with Phillips Petroleum, he maintained an avid interest in company affairs, and all that was needed to keep fully informed was to cross the street to Frank's house where a willing and admiring brother lived.

7

CIVIC LEADER

Lee Eldas Phillips had many lives, all intertwined but somehow uniquely separate from each other. The common threads which ran through his activities were pride, a deep sense of loyalty to family, friends, and business interests, and an unselfish urge to make his world a better place in which to live—through unremunerated service. He not only was a philanthropist, but also he gave generously of his time and knowledge to a plethora of community, state, and national activities.

His son Philip recalls with great pride the heavy commitment L. E. made to community affairs. "Father was a civic leader," he once said. "He worked so hard for Bartlesville and Oklahoma at times that he had to neglect his business responsibilities."[1] Few men can afford such freedom of time; still fewer men have the ability or command the respect required to lead entire communities to lofty and unrealized dreams. Lee Eldas Phillips had the freedom and the verve to accomplish great civic goals. His was an enviable record.

Such men begin their service because it is their nature to serve. At the time it seems "the thing to do," or is rationalized by a shrug of the shoulders and a time-worn cliche: "Well, somebody has to do it." Only in later years, after there is time for reflection and philosophizing, are they able to describe what motivated them to become community builders. What actually happens is that they are born gregarious, unselfish people with a vision of what must be done and the will to accomplish it. That characterized L. E. Phillips when he moved to Bartlesville, Indian Territory, in 1905: a self-motivated, uncomplicated individual who led because he was born to lead. Later, when he could put the words to it, he was equally as uncomplicated in explaining his motivation: a man owes more to his community than just his taxes.

The rest of his philosophy of service is beautifully simple, the words sometimes borrowed to be sure, but nonetheless unique to the man, Lee Eldas Phillips. "He profits most who serves best," he was fond of saying, and often added, "We are all, more or less, our brother's keeper and should give willingly of our service in the interests of the general welfare." Another favorite was, "If you are a clock watcher, you will not succeed in life."

There was more. "Too many people are merely passive in their community efforts." And when he was moved to soap box oratory, for which he had few peers, he would say, "I would enjoy spending the rest of my life, if possible, for the good of others. I am proud of my American citizenship and gladly assume the duties such citizenship entails." Had he not been living proof of his words, mockery would have been his lot rather than the enormous respect which everyone showered on him.[2]

When he first came to establish permanent residence in Bartlesville, the town had already begun to develop a municipal consciousness. A railroad, first begun by local investors and later completed by the Santa Fe, had reached the city in 1899. City elections were held that year, and a mayor, city recorder, and five aldermen were elected by a total vote of 50. The First National Bank, later to be owned by the Phillips brothers, opened in 1900, and a telephone system was installed in 1901. A Commercial Club, forerunner of the Chamber of Commerce, was formed in June of 1904, and George B. Keeler, one of the early founders of the city, was chosen president. In rapid order a water works system was completed in November of 1904, a volunteer fire company was formed with Dr. F. N. Black as chief in December, and a sewer system was installed in 1905. Street paving also began in that year. Retail stores, homes, schools, and churches already rounded out a budding municipality of some 2000 souls.[3]

Lee was looking for a way to help his city when he arrived, and an opportunity to serve came early for him. After Congress passed the Oklahoma Enabling Act in June of 1906, Mayor W. T. Sidell of Bartlesville proclaimed Tuesday, June 19, to be "Statehood Day" and appointed a committee of leading citizens to plan an appropriate celebration, with himself as chairman and the recently-arrived L. E. Phillips as secretary. Businesses were closed at 6 p.m. by order of the mayor "in order that they may take part in the demonstration"; fireworks were banned because of the potential fire hazard, but plenty of noise was provided by shooting anvils, and the public was "expected to join in to increase the volume of noise." Speeches by city founders George B. Keeler, William Johnstone, and Colonel John N. Florer, as well as Mayor Sidell, highlighted the occasion. Said one of them, "The gleam of the 46th star in the firmament of American Statehood is at last seen clear and steady above the horizon."[4] The celebration was a huge success, but statehood would not officially be established until November 16, 1907, a date which would then become the official "Statehood Day."

L. E. by then had established himself and had gained acceptance from those already at work. There was plenty for a natural leader to do. With rail transportation and an increasing supply of natural gas flowing from newly drilled wells, a concerted effort was needed to attract industries compatible with natural resources and consumer needs. The task of attracting new businesses fell to the Commercial Club, and L. E. quickly became associated with that organization soon after the successful opening of the Citizens Bank and Trust Company.

He was assigned to a special committee to work with Dee Lanyon of Neodesha, Kansas, and other members of his family in an effort to bring a smelting plant to Bartlesville. With adequate rail transportation to bring ore from Missouri and Kansas and an abundant supply of natural gas to fire the furnaces, Bartlesville seemed a logical site for the Lanyons. They agreed. Following a massive effort to effect favorable rates from railroads and natural gas producers and to raise money for purchasing the site for the smelter, the deal was consummated in August, 1906. The Commercial Club, with L. E. as acting secretary, had pulled off a coup, and the town would attract still more smelting firms in the future. The Club's worth to the city was firmly established, as was L. E.'s value to it.[5]

At the next election of officers, L. E. was elected to head the Club, and in accepting the presidency he "exhibited the spirit that will serve to make the accomplishments of the Club for the [coming] year greater than those of any previous twelve months." Much can be accomplished, Lee said, but it would take something besides "hot air." "What is needed," he added, "is a waking up to the necessity of contributing of time." Phillips called for every man to be a "booster"; "knockers" should find some other employment.[6]

With amazing speed, the new president moved his townsmen. By late February, another smelter was headed for Bartlesville, a new creamery was assured, and contracts with the Southwestern Chautauqua had provided the city with prominent speakers as well as half the proceeds from admissions. A road committee was established "to look after the roads and bridges leading into the city," one member of which was H. H. McClintock, who would become a life-long friend to L. E.[7]

Moving with the rising spirit he was generating, L.

E. urged the formation of a Booster Club to keep the enthusiasm of the citizens high and to advertise the city. A Booster's Banquet was arranged for February 28, 1907, to "kick the drive off." A slogan, "I can, I will— Bartlesville," was adopted, and everyone, including ladies, was invited to contribute one dollar and attend the banquet. It was "a signal success, a feast of reason and flow of the soul." More than 200 "Boosters" crowded into the banquet room and roared with approval as speaker after speaker called them to action. What was happening was almost imperceptible at the time, but a young, recently arrived Moses was about to lead his people out of the wilderness.[8]

Never had enthusiasm been so strong, never had so great a percentage of total citizens been involved in building and boosting the town. L. E. was quoted or at least mentioned almost daily in the local press as the dynamic leader of the Commercial Club. In the short span of a year, his name had become a household word, and he was encouraged to continue in his role as head of the Club for another term. Of his activities, he took the greatest pride in helping to plan and complete an interurban electric rail service between Bartlesville and nearby Dewey. "Bartlesville is growing so fast that the ordinary means of [transportation] no longer answer the purpose," he said. "We can't wait along the road until some farmer's wagon comes by . . . . We need some means of transportation that will carry us to Dewey or around the city in a short time." The town agreed: 2500 people turned out to witness the driving of the first spike. And in June, he launched a campaign for civic development, for paving of streets, and for other public improvements. L. E. had the town moving; the people "had a mind to work," and their achievements were increasing. Unlike countless other small oil towns throughout the Midwest, Bartlesville seemed determined to rise above a roustabout's village and become a resident's ha-

In this carriage, L.E. was arrested and fined for driving over a fireman's hose which was being used to battle a raging house fire. The rider here is Martha Jane, his daughter.

ven, thanks in large measure to a young former Iowan in their midst.[9]

L. E. saw the Club through its second annual Booster Banquet, then declined to accept reelection to the presidency in 1909. He continued to be active and very supportive of its efforts. Despite his surging popularity he made a tactical error on March 22, 1910, which brought about his arrest. While driving his buggy home, he approached an area where firemen were busily fighting a blazing house. Perhaps deep in thought, but warned nonetheless not to drive over the firemen's hoses, he did so and was arrested and charged with interfering with fire officers in the line of duty. Although his lawyer contended there was no ordinance against driving over a fire hose, L. E. pled guilty and was fined $11.75. Returning to the bank, L. E. sent a porter to the police station with a check in that amount, instructing him to obtain a receipt from the judge. "You tell L. E.," the judge roared to the porter, "that being loose is receipt enough." An examination of the check, still extant in a family scrapbook, shows the word "experience" written in as explanation for the expenditure.[10]

Service to the community in a variety of ways followed. He was appointed to a board of city park commissioners and, with his usual energy, urged a program of cleaning up the city's parks and recreation areas. He also recommended that prisoners be used to perform that work. Later he was elected to the board of directors of a new country club and was asked to help select a suitable construction site. The club, named Oak Hill, opened formally with a banquet and dance on November 27, 1911. It was the culmination of a long dream for some residents of Bartlesville.[11]

Undoubtedly because of his service to Bartlesville and his growing visibility throughout banking circles, he received strong support in 1914 for appointment to the Federal Reserve Board in Kansas City. That he failed to be named to the position certainly was not because Oklahomans failed to endorse him. It was just one of life's cobblestones that had to await marking at a later date. No enthusiasm was lost; he later served admirably on the committee formed to plan a Gala Day program to dedicate the new Bartlesville Court House on April 11, 1915, and he was appointed to membership on the Boy Scout Council, an organization to which he became firmly attached because he believed it highly beneficial for young boys.[12]

Banking responsibilities, connected with his service to the Oklahoma Bankers Association, filled much of his extracurricular time during 1916 and 1917, and brought him into a close working relationship with Oklahoma political and civic leaders. As the war in Europe wore on, much attention was drawn to America's possible involvement in it. As president of the OBA, L. E. frequently was asked to participate in conferences to discuss

L.E. had genuine respect for the Indian population in Oklahoma. Here he is shown with a group of them at Woolaroc, Frank's ranch retreat.

topics related to the war. Building up agricultural preparedness became a theme of the OBA in 1917, and a program was begun to prevent food shortages should large numbers of farm workers be drafted into service.[13]

When war came for Americans in April of 1917, new efforts were required of civic leaders. L. E. first was asked to serve as chairman of the finance committee of the local Red Cross. Bartlesville and Washington County were being asked to raise $25,000 as a part of a national Red Cross drive to support our fighting men in Europe. As was his style, L.E. called for cummunity-wide meetings in local school houses on June 16; at these he and area ministers attempted to explain the need and rally support for the county fund drive.[14] The response was excellent. By June 19 a total of $71,340.49 had been raised as "Red Cross fund solicitors were greeted with open purses by citizens of the whole county." As a corollary to that effort, a Liberty Loan drive was waged in Bartlesville, aided by local Boy Scouts in a door-to-door bond selling campaign. Some $478,400 in Liberty Bonds were sold by June 15, after which L. E. inevitably was drawn into the activity. By October the sum had reached a million dollars for Washington County, L. E. having "quit work" to take active charge of the campaign in Bartlesville.[15]

By November, there was a new and broader assignment, this time as state chairman of the national Red Cross Christmas membership drive. To lead the effort, L. E. opened an office in Oklahoma City and assumed responsibility for a region which included Oklahoma and the Texas Panhandle. It was a drive to recruit "more people than money." Membership would allow individuals "to become affiliated with war activities." The slogan adopted was, "Let the boys at the front know you care."[16] Phillips crisscrossed the state, addressing groups of citizens and exhorting campaign workers. He sought "to recruit an army" of one dollar donors, a fee set to allow everyone to join. It was, he said, "a glorious opportunity, a wonderful privilege to serve. I never knew what real fun and happiness was until I got into this work."[17] With an excellent state and regional organization and with Christmas approaching for American soldiers in France, the people of Oklahoma and the Texas Panhandle responded admirably. The original quota was set at 190,000 members; L. E. raised that figure to 500,000, a challenge which was itself exceeded in the end. Coining a new and catchy slogan, "All you need is a heart and a dollar," L. E. drove his campaign machinery to achieve 750,000 memberships, a high for the entire nation. Their slogan later was adopted by the National Red Cross. He and his workers were praised by the national chairman for their efforts.[18]

A proud and happy L. E. was not given much time to relax following that effort. Indeed, almost immediately he was asked to address a group which would plan a new Liberty Loan drive. And he continued to travel the state to assist local Red Cross organizations in their war work. He also returned to business activities, but by

April he was "back in harness" again, this time as Chairman of Oklahoma's Red Cross War Fund Campaign, with a goal of $1,660,000. Because of the national publicity he had received during the Christmas drive, he was immediately challenged by J. E. Johnson, who had just been appointed chairman of the campaign in Missouri. A wire from Johnson stated that he was feeling very cocky and wished to bet L. E. $100 that Missouri "would exceed her quota by a larger percentage than the state of Oklahoma."[19]

That was all L. E. needed to get going. The old war horse responded to Johnson, saying that, by his interpretation, it was not a bet because "my money is on a sure thing." Throughout April, L. E. set his house in order, made plans to reopen his Oklahoma City office, and reassembled a statewide organization. On May 4, Phillips could report that "the whole state is well organized and is full of enthusiasm." He predicted state's quota would be oversubscribed. Dates for the drive were set for May 20-27.[20]

More than a membership drive, the War Fund Campaign was directed at raising monies to help Red Cross workers on distant battlefields to tend wounds and minister to the needs of American soldiers. The campaign had a powerful appeal, and a true patriot, L. E. Phillips, enthusiastically led the charge. "Fight with your dollars," he urged Oklahomans; "meet the canvassers halfway . . . . Loose change won't do. When some fellows are giving lives, or possibly arms and legs, it is not sufficient for us to give three cheers."[21]

Phillips again conducted a personal speaking campaign as well as directed a statewide organization. He used every conceivable means of communicating, urging and cajoling his coworkers. He especially made heavy use of the telegraph, prompting one writer in Ottawa to suggest that if he would donate to the Red Cross all the money he spent in sending telegrams, the association would be greatly benefited. Lee was "entertained" by the letter, and promptly wired the writer, "I still claim the war made Ottawa County rich," a statement to which his precursor earlier had apparently taken offense.[22]

It was a difficult, almost enervating campaign, made so by a maddeningly short deadline. However, after periods of pessimism and optimism, it was revealed that things were going well. At closing time on May 27, the figure stood at $2,041,477. "This has been a hard job," L. E. told his managers, "and I personally appreciate your efforts and compliment you on the results." He then concluded, "Whatever we do now, however, we shall not match the sacrifice our allies and soldiers have made, or that which the boys we are sending to the front must endure."[23]

There is no record revealing if L. E. won the "bet" with the Missouri chairman, but he had done very well indeed.

There was no rest for the weary. He was approached immediately to head a campaign for the Red Cross, which desperately needed trained nurses for service in Europe. He accepted and set about developing a speaker's program to tour the state and to urge registered nurses to volunteer for overseas service. A short time later he accepted the task of heading the Fourth Liberty Loan Campaign in Oklahoma. It was a different type of challenge, one he accepted with enthusiasm. Instead of trying to solicit cash contributions, he now had a commodity to sell which represented a good investment in the form of interest-bearing bonds.[24]

In late August, it was reported that L. E. was "pushing forward the plans for opening the drive," although he did not as yet have an announced quota from the nation's capital. Because of the importance of the campaign, state officials had provided him with spacious quarters in the east wing of the capitol. And as a gesture of encouragement, A. M. McKinney, Secretary of the

State School Land Department told the press that the land commission would invest $651,000 in Liberty Bonds, one dollar for each child of school age in Oklahoma. A fine beginning.[25]

As the drive took shape, L. E. was paid high compliments by *The Investor* on September 19, 1918. "Mr. Phillips," the editorial read,

> came into national prominence, it might be said, as the Oklahoma director of two Red Cross drives that were extraordinarily successful. He adopted methods of such merit and conducted the campaigns with such splendid executive ability and showed such resourcefulness that the government selected him as the man to superintendent Oklahoma's drive in the vast loan campaign now underway in this state. He is a genius in organization and in management of the succeeding activity of that organization.

Genius though he was in organizing fund drives, it seems incredible that he was able to sustain his enthusiasm and energy. Yet he tackled a third major campaign with the same zest that characterized all his efforts. Great strides were made to organize every county as all waited the announcement of the state's quota. It came on September 25, and the opening date for the campaign was set for October 7: $38,841,700 was to be raised in a "whirlwind campaign of two weeks."[26]

Lee Eldas confidently predicted on October 4 that "half the quota is now in sight," the result of reports on work done in advance by county chairmen and individuals throughout the state.[27] Yet despite early expressions of optimism, the struggle was fierce. Bells and sirens may have signaled the beginning of the campaign on October 7, but L. E. and his chief advisors had to "beat the drums" every step of the way. Rumors that the war soon would end; influenza, which humbled some communities; and general reluctance on the part of certain "big interests" in larger cities made the work difficult. On October 19, after a two-week solicitation and "after having overcome the most serious obstacles that could possibly arise to handicap the campaign," state chairman Phillips announced that a total subscription of $39,-250,000 had been raised.[28]

Phillips said, in retrospect, that it was "absolutely the hardest campaign the state ever had. Raising $39 million loomed as an impossibility until a late hour." Co-workers agreed; the state committee praised him and presented him a bronze honor badge, "an award for good service."[29] He was deserving of it—and much, much more.

He had but time to draw a deep breath before he plunged back into another drive, accepting again the state chairmanship of the Red Cross Christmas Drive. The morale of American boys overseas and the wounded, he said, were "crying for help from home." The war was over, but the suffering had not ended. L. E. could not let them down. It was time for a roll call of those who had given before, and a time to summon new members to the cause.[30]

Although the Roll Call Drive was scheduled for December 16 to 23, "two sacred hours" were to be set aside on December 18, between the hours of 9 to 11 o'clock in the morning, during which time business all across the state would be suspended and every man, woman, and child would remain indoors so that they could be readily available to canvassing volunteers. L. E. set as his goal a total of one million members, and again used the slogan of 1918: "A heart and a dollar."[31] A major effort was made, but apathy cooled the drive. The armistice in Europe evoked complacency at home. The final tabulation fell far short of the announced goal; indeed, the numbers were less than those for 1918.[32]

Few men in Oklahoma had given so unselfishly of themselves and their time for so worthy a cause. L. E.

supported the war because he believed in the cause—making the world safe for democracy, the bedrock on which a great nation and a free enterprise economy was based. Following this prolonged period of almost exclusive civic service, he returned to Bartlesville, resigned as chief operating officer of the Bartlesville National Bank, and plunged full-time into the petroleum business with his brother. His civic responsibilities thereafter were conducted as complements to his business activities.

It was inevitable that one so visible in times of great public fund raising campaigns would be mentioned for political office. Perhaps the strongest move ever made to involve him in state politics came soon after the highly successful Red Cross Christmas Membership Campaign of 1917. Little known in the state at large until that drive, he "woke up the natives," and people across the state began to ask, "Who is this man Phillips?"[33] Word went out that he was one of the most active men in his city, always "in the trenches in every move that means something better for Bartlesville." He and brother Frank "dig down in their pockets" more often than any other men in their town for public enterprises, it was said. Such praise served only to spread rumors that Lee might be enticed to a new level of public service. "Did you ever hear a political bee buzz around your head?" a newsman asked him one day at his bank. Without shuffling the stack of papers in front of him, L. E. responded, "I have never been in politics and I don't want to get in."[34]

"But suppose your friends should force you into the race?" the reporter continued. No response came and the journalist was left to his own interpretation of the silence. But he wrote positively about L. E.'s excellent qualifications. "He is a successful businessman, has an abundance of good common sense, and, *if elected governor* [italics supplied], would give the people a real business administration."

The bee would buzz around his bonnet periodically

L.E. at Woolaroc (hat under arm) with a group of civic workers.

throughout his active business career, but politics held
little attraction for Lee Phillips. Not even the opportunity to become governor-general of the Philippines was
of such significance as to cause him to leave his beloved
Bartlesville or his revered Oklahoma.

Across the years Lee joined several civic organizations and clubs, each of which performed a public service
of some type. During World War I he became a member
of the Washington County Council for Defense and was
later appointed by the governor of Oklahoma to the
State Council for Defense. He was also a founder, with
others, of an organization known as the International
Police. He held membership in several social and/or
country clubs, among them being Hillcrest (Bartlesville),
Paris County, Tulsa, and Fort Worth. He belonged to
the Rotary and Kiwanis clubs, the Elks and Moose
lodges, and on March 7, 1907, was one of the organizers
of the Royal Arch Masons in Bartlesville. He ultimately
became a 32nd degree Mason.

One annual function, sponsored by brother Frank, featured the reunion of thieves and robbers at Woolaroc. This photograph shows the five Phillips brothers during one of the annual affairs.

Active for many years in his church, the First Christian Church of Bartlesville, he served as a deacon and chairman of the Board of Trustees. Although he never taught Bible classes, he taught by example and leadership. He was generous with his time as well as his money. He enjoyed a very close relationship with his minister, the Reverend Harry Ice, and through him aided many people and causes. As Reverend Ice worded it in 1929, "[I have] handled literally thousands of dollars in the last five years. This work has been done quietly, many times the recipients not knowing the source of their help. This work has been done in the name of the church. It is his conviction that the church ought to do more of this kind of work . . . ."[35]

Lee Phillips loved his children and his grandchildren, whom he gathered about him at 1201 Cherokee Street whenever he could. But he also was concerned about the children of others, and that led him into other types of service. He supported the Boy Scouts liberally and served as president of the Bartlesville YMCA and later as a board member of the Oklahoma State YMCA. He also served as an officer in the Oklahoma Chamber of Commerce. And because his two sons were graduates of the University of Kansas, he was a donor to, as well as a director of, the University of Kansas Endowment Association. He was a regent for the University of Tulsa, from which he received an honorary doctor's degree, and he was awarded other honorary degrees from Washburn, Kansas Wesleyan, and Phillips universities.

As an avid Republican, he contributed materially to his party, and on occasion was approached to become an active candidate for local, state, and national offices, a temptation he resisted because he had little interest in pure politics. He was a close acquaintance of Herbert Hoover, probably through his friend Patrick Hurley, and he spent several evenings at the White House at various functions, many times with Node also a participant.

Because of his friendship with Kansas Governor Alfred M. Landon, he became active in the presidential campaign of 1936, traveling far and wide in fund raising efforts and making speeches for his candidate. This association brought the two men and their families even closer together, and they were frequent visitors to each other's homes and occasional vacationers at seasonal retreats. He also was an active participant in the Wendell Wilkie campaign in 1940.

Perhaps Lee Eldas Phillips' life of public service came at a time in history when attitudes toward business were more positive and trusting, when businessmen were regarded as the architects of the future. This is almost a forgotten era, a time when business leaders were more highly respected as models for ambitious youth to emulate and as captains for willing community builders to

The beginning and end of a career. This photograph, taken on the day of his retirement from Phillips Petroleum Company in April, 1933, also shows L.E. as he left home to become a salesman in Iowa.

follow. That he came along at the right time and in the right business setting was fortuitous both for Bartlesville and Oklahoma—and for America. A large part of his heart was reserved for his fellowman, and he opened it, without thought of compensation or in search of accolades, in an effort to build his community. In so doing, he made the state and nation a better place for himself as well as for those he served.

8

RETIREMENT YEARS

The year 1933, from the standpoint of health, was not kind to Lee Phillips. Nervousness, brought on by excessive high blood pressure, and stomach disorders, which altered his diet and caused him to lose weight, made his routine business responsibilities grow less and less attractive. For his entire life, L. E. had never been a bench warmer, but substitutes increasingly were obliged to handle his duties. That, plus the constant and affectionate urgings of his sensitive family to consider "slowing down," finally convinced him to accept retirement with dignity.

The transition to private life may have been difficult for L. E., but if it was, there are neither records nor recollections which indicate anything other than satisfaction that the decision finally was made—and at a time, hopefully, when a slower pace would permit maximum enjoyment of the affluence he had accumulated. Wealth though he had, he conducted himself in the enjoyment of it in such a way that none would have classified him as a conspicuous consumer.

L. E. was not like Alexander the Great who wept because he had run out of new worlds to conquer; he was more like Dr. Panglois who cheered because he already lived in the best of all possible worlds. Indeed, as late as 1939 he was telling the graduating class at Washburn College that "there are still frontiers to be conquered," that great though the advances had been in his lifetime, the "possibilities of the future are still greater than any yet realized."[1]

One wonders if the company felt he was actually gone, for it took the firm a year to send him the resolution adopted by the Board praising him upon his retirement.[2] Lee still was needed as a consultant to the firm, and he stayed in demand as a speaker for many years because he was one of the most knowledgeable men in the oil industry. Retirement merely allowed him to be more selective in what he did, and it freed him from feelings of guilt when he refused an invitation. From the scope of his interests and the volume of his activities, it becomes difficult to label the period after April of 1934 as "the retirement years." More properly it might be designated as the "I did it my way" years.

Specifically, he continued in useful service to others, but he took time to pursue neglected hobbies, enjoy an increased schedule of traveling, associate more often with revered friends, and tend more carefully to his infirmities. He also spent more quality time with his children and his grandchildren, watching the latter grow to maturity, marry, and start lives of their own. The last ten years were busy, fun-filled years even as his health worsened.[3]

One of the areas of service which brought him great happiness derived from a quasi hobby he enjoyed. For years he had owned a farm, and on occasion he gave considerable attention to its development. During the business years at Phillips, he more often used it as an escape valve than as a recreational device. Now in his retirement years, he turned to the farm for a partial fulfillment of the void he experienced when he left the regimenting schedule he kept at Phillips.

He not only beautified the farm with substantive and aesthetic improvements, but also he took seriously to raising Poland China hogs and White-faced Hereford cattle, and to growing award-winning pecans in a care-

At his Philson Farms, L.E. sought relaxation and diversion in part by riding his favorite horse, Robert Lee, a three-gaited sorrel.

fully pruned grove. The pecans he used most often as gifts to special friends and organizations. The number of people who received shipments of them at Christmas each year was extensive, and none who received them but praised him lavishly for his gesture. But it was in the area of livestock that his community service was allowed to flourish.

With his son, Phil, who also had cultivated a strong interest in developing registered livestock, the two embarked on an elaborate program of breeding, raising, selling, and showing Poland China hogs.[4] Countless times in contest and show arenas, the Phillips' animals garnered prizes in a tremendously competitive field. And their activity in hogs expanded their interests into related areas, especially into local and regional 4-H Club activities. L. E. frequently had the youthful stock raisers as his guests for official picnics, and on one such occasion a total of 700 "future farmers" invaded the farm for fun and food, which he underwrote. An interesting sidelight to this joint undertaking with Phil resulted in naming the country estate Philson Farms, which referred to both L. E. and his son.[5]

L. E. enjoyed speaking and was as entertaining as he was knowledgeable. One Tulsa newsman wrote that Lee Phillips "might have been the bard of Bartlesville if he hadn't gone into oil and banking."[6] He was in demand by both industries, the one because of his vast experience, the other because he was a director on the Board of the Federal Reserve Bank of Kansas City, the only regular involvement he retained after his retirement. He spoke at such important functions as the dedication ceremonies for the reopening of the Missouri River Valley to river traffic, a part of the Inland Waterways Commission project which Patrick Hurley had initiated.[7]

Within petroleum associations during these years he became the elder statesman. His frequent appearances and his ringing attacks on federal oil policies and taxation of the industry extended his contacts in a very significant way within the industry that had made him wealthy. As late as 1941, he was still being quoted as an authority on the role oil would play in World War II.[8]

Another hobby which he revived in 1934, due to the influence of Will Rogers, was the collection of Wooden Indians, which once were traditional fixtures at tobacco shops and drug stores. These hand-carved statues became collectors' items as old-fashioned country stores gradually gave way to modern grocery and general purpose stores, and Will had asked Lee to help locate one. One fireplace mantel from the home at 1201 Cherokee, which sported several carved Indian faces, was removed when the home was sold and placed in a museum room at the splendid ranch-style home that Philip Rex built and occupied on the old country estate.[9] Lee's interest in preserving another part of the American heritage led him to assemble an ideal set of McGuffey's Readers,

One of L.E.'s closest friends was Kansas Governor Alf Landon (pipe in hand) with whom he vacationed frequently. Here L.E. and Landon are shown with a friend, Henry North, (second from left) in Florida in 1938.

school readers which "historians claim . . . did more to shape the thought and culture" of his and previous generations than "any other influence." The rare collection included some of the earliest editions.[10]

The art of Isaac Walton, fishing, was also a source of much pleasure to L. E., and he was seldom without his camera when a picture could confirm an angler's story. There appears infrequently in his scrapbooks a type of handwritten calendar showing each day's catch, verified by the signatures of his fishing companions. Such entries were another side of Lee's humor; no one could ever accuse him of exaggerating his successes or "telling about the one that got away." Ironically, it was

Not always the winning angler, here Node displays her 15-pound kingfish, L.E. his one-pound mackeral in Florida, March, 1938.

during a fishing trip to Canada in 1935 that the press began to identify him as the retired chairman of the executive committee at Phillips Petroleum.[11] One of his frequent fishing buddies was Kansas Governor Alf Landon. They were close friends, having been "young men together in the oil business in Kansas and Oklahoma," and the two men and their wives spent a few long vacation/fishing retreats together. In 1936, L. E. served as host to the unsuccessful Republican Presidential Candidate on one occasion at Monticello, Florida. Landon recalled one story about that trip.[12]

This one is for the books, said Governor Landon.

Phillips drops in to see me at Topeka, up in Kansas, some weeks ago. Tells me all about this fishing camp of his at Monticello, Florida. Tells me the big-mouth bass you call "green trout" down South here are so thick in the river that they've formed a suicide club and fight for the chance to get caught. Tells how he lowers the stage of the river everytime he goes fishing, he takes so many fish out of the stream. Tells me we'll eat fish until we get tired of fish, and I know nobody ever gets tired of big-mouth bass with bacon.

And then this morning we walk out of the [hotel] and step into Phillips' car . . . , and I stumble over something on the floor, and look down at it . . . and what do you think it is? Canned salmon!

When asked about the episode, L. E. had the grace to blush and admit it, chuckling, "I like fish, and there isn't always time to get out your tackle and catch some."[13] Landon and Phillips loved teasing and arguing with each other, especially on outings where they could relax. They were to fish together in the picturesque western Yellowstone and Jackson Hole areas in the summer of 1939.[14]

Taking major excursions always had held attraction for L. E. and Node. Both of them at times traveled for their health. They also used every opportunity to travel together, taking their children when possible in order to make up for their periods of enforced separation. An overview of their out-of-country travel is interesting. They took two world cruises (1930 and 1937), two Caribbean excursions (1923 and 1938), two European junkets (1922 and 1928), two Hawaiian holidays (1921 and 1926), and two Mexico City tours (1925 and 1938). Only two of the major undertakings occurred after his retirement, but they were truly major trips: a world cruise and an extravagant swing through Europe. When single trips to Canada (1913) and Alaska (1920) are added to that list, it makes the scope of their traveling all the more impressive, given the fact that Lee would not fly and

*L.E. loved to travel. Here he is shown with a group in Rome
in August, 1922, just after they had had an audience with the
Pope. L to R: Martha Jane, Bob Brewer, L.E., Jr., L.E., Node,
Mrs. R.P. Brewer, R.P. Brewer, Susan Kelley (the Phillips'
housekeeper), Philip Rex.*

thus was obliged to use surface transportation.[15] Ships
and trains were his forte; often he would have his chauffeur drive his car to a destination while he and Node
rode the train.

Two principal things motivated Lee's desire to travel.
First, it is obvious that health was primary. During one
European junket in 1928, he wrote members of the
Anchor Club a revealing insight into his basic physical
problem:

> As to myself, I do feel better at times, but still have
> days and nights when I don't know what the matter
> is . . . . I am like the old [slave] who was asked by his
> doctor to describe his symptoms and he said, "Boss,
> I eats well and I sleeps well but somehow I can't get

Node riding an elephant in Ceylon in 1937.

any appetite for work." That I think pretty well describes my case. When I behave myself, my blood pressure and nerves act pretty well, but if I don't then I *blow up.* I have been mighty good now for two months, and I suppose if I keep it up I will be normal. But it will be a slow process and pretty darned lonesome then. I can't help but wonder about the business and things which don't help. But remember it is pretty

The Phillips astride camels in Egypt in 1937.

hard to suddenly change your entire method of living
. . . . The answer to our traveling around is I just can't
sit down and twaddle my thumbs.[16]

Health was a prime motivator, but fantasy was also
a factor. A Bartlesville newsman interviewed Lee on his
return from a two-month sojourn in Hawaii in 1921,
and reported that Phillips had started out five years
before "on a program to see America and its possessions
first"—and that he seemed to be working regularly at
the task of fulfilling that dream. Ever the dedicated
sightseer, L. E. always had his own camera along to record and preserve the wonders that he saw for his own
enjoyment.[17]

On every trip there were fun-filled experiences,
from being photographed with "some of my girls"
(nearly bare-chested hula dancers in Hawaii) in 1939,
to playfully raising money to foment a revolution in
Mexico. The latter escapade happened while he was in
route to Los Angeles in 1921 to attend the American
Bankers Convention. Riding a train with several banking
friends, they took a side trip into Juárez, Mexico, during

L.E. and Node at the Taj Mahal in 1937.

a stopover in El Paso. Unhappy because there was no bullfight scheduled for that day, he and Bob Brewer raised $140 with which "to raise an insurrection." They could not agree upon who should lead it, so the money "was invested in muscatel to avoid income tax collectors and customs officials." Whatever became of this Mexican inspiration was a closely held secret, but the entire train came into Los Angeles singing, "How Dry I Am."[18]

Lee made numerous friends all over the world and engaged in note exchanges with many of them. One of those who remembered him was Manual Quezon, President of the Philippine Islands after 1937, whom he first met in 1930. During his world cruise that year, Lee briefly made a survey of banking and economic conditions in Manila for the Hoover administration. He met Quezon and became a fast friend. A Christmas telegram in 1941 from Quezon, while his country was being occupied by the Japanese, was a cherished possession which Lee shared with a local reporter, who then re-

L.E. with "some of the girls" in Hawaii in 1939.

vealed more of the attending conversation than Phillips
had intended. "We may get in Dutch," the newsman
wrote, "for the remarks which follow because L. E. Phillips does not like publicity. But we think he should not
be too mad if we told this one thing: If overwork had
not caught up with him he would have been made governor general of the Philippines . . . ." That fact was one
of Lee's most carefully guarded secrets for more than
a decade.[19]

Cherished though such acquaintances were, Lee revered most those American friends who shared his type
of humor. Alf Landon's wit and light-hearted reparte
always cheered Lee and obliged him to keep his epee
"en guarde." Their sharp exchanges, always in fun and
respect, were the measure of true friendship. Amon
Carter, a prominent Texas philanthropist, also enjoyed

Dining at the Royal Hawaiian Hotel in 1939.

a lively tete-a-tete with Lee. Some of the gifts they exchanged bordered on the ribald, but each roared his approval and acceptance of all gifts, no matter how bizzare.[20]

Humorist Irving S. Cobb also engaged in funny, written exchanges with Lee, once complaining when he received a shipment of pecans which were unshelled. He had suggested to Lee that he make "the little woman tend to her [hulling] work." Lee's excuse was that he had been puny, and "my woman has been so busy chopping wood, husking corn, whittling and making sausage and chittlings that she just ain't had time to do this for you."[21] Such friends added spice to life.

Lee, Oklahoma, and the entire nation suffered a blow when another close friend, humorist Will Rogers, and aviator Wiley Post crashed to their deaths on August 16, 1935, near Point Barrow, Alaska. Post was an experienced pilot who twice had flown around the world, and he had conducted high altitude flights sponsored by Phillips Petroleum to test fuel and equipment. He was beloved by everyone and refused to let his patched eye reflect adversely on his hazardous occupation. He

L.E. being presented with a 150-year-old bottle of sherry by a Dr. Bostwich in Gibraltar in 1937.

and Rogers were on the first leg of a globe-circling tour when tragedy struck.[22]

Rogers, with his easy, unsophisticated mannerisms and his keen sense of humor, was one of Lee's favorite people. Theirs was a friendship which grew as L. E. began to emerge as one of the titans of the Oklahoma oil industry. For almost two decades Rogers would take time to visit with Lee in his home when his travels brought him to Oklahoma. Always when they were together, an easy-flow humor resulted. On one of these visits, as previously mentioned, Rogers signed his name on a wooden hearth plate at 1201 Cherokee in 1929, a signature which was then burned into the wood for permanency.[23]

The exchanges between the two men during the last months before the fatal accident attest to their closeness. Sometime before Christmas in 1934, L. E. bought two Wooden Indians and sent one of them to Rogers' home in Santa Monica, California. Rogers acknowledged the gift in a lengthy telegram, saying, "The Indian couldn't

Will Rogers, a native of Claremore, Oklahoma, a close friend, is shown with L.E. and others at Woolaroc.

have arrived at a more opportune time. Amon Carter had us all just talked ragged, so I just switched him over to the chief. Now the Indian is kicking and says him or Amon has to leave."[24] Phillips had found the stern-faced Indian, dubbed "Chief Sour Puss," in Roger's home town of Claremore, and Will promised to make him grin with one of his jokes, "the one about the Republican Party." Rogers could not resist the dig at Phillips' party affiliation.[25]

During the summer of 1935, Rogers and Post vacationed in New Mexico, briefly visited with Waite Phillips, and stopped at the famous Vermejo Ranch. "Wiley is fishing, and I am looking out at the cattle," Will wrote to the *Kansas City Star* on July 16, just a few weeks before his tragic death.[26] Then on August 10, Lee wired Will in Juneau, Alaska, from his vacation site in Poland Spring, Maine, addressing him as "Sourdough Will Rogers":

Amon Carter (far right), powerful Fort Worth publisher, also was a close friend. Here he "arrests" L.E. and Frank as they arrive in his city to attend a dinner.

You and Wiley watch your step, you don't loose your ship or miss the last boat or go native . . . . Bartlesville Horse Show October second to fifth. Mrs. Phillips joins me in invitation to you and your woman to be our house guests. All the old timers will be there including Amon Carter. Make your plans accordingly.[27]

No further messages came from Will. He would be unable to accept the invitation to attend the horse show and joke one more time with old friends. Friends everywhere eulogized Rogers. Irving S. Cobb said, "He was a friend to all the world. Men like him, I'm sure, don't come along oftener than once in a century."[28] Lee Phillips sadly commented that he was "stunned so completely

L.E., Ed, and Frank on their trip of nostalgia to Iowa in 1941.

that I cannot get over it." He wired Mrs. Rogers a short message of deepest sympathy.[29]

The loss of a friend made an aging Lee Phillips more determined to enjoy those who still lived. In October of 1937 he made a nostalgic return to the place of his birth, taking photographs of a variety of people, buildings, and locations which in his mind represented those cobblestones on which he had left his imprint in his earlier life. Touching those "stones" and reminiscing about "those days" were important to him, and always had been. He even walked an old railroad track where as a boy he had helped his friends grease the rails in order to frustrate the locomotive engineers. And there was A. E. Lake, still living in Bedford, Iowa, the man on whose farm he had dug potatoes for ten cents a day. It was a grand, soul-filling visit. A few years later, in September of 1941, L. E. repeated the trip, this time with two of his brothers, Frank and Ed. Together they stopped in Conway, Creston, Gravity, and Bedford, as if returning

L.E., Ed, and Frank in Gravity, Iowa, in September, 1941, at the gravesite of their parents.

to sacred shrines to worship. They walked by the old swimming hole, chatted with relatives and old friends, and talked about some boyhood activities which by then had become either suspect in accuracy or apocryphal.[30]

L. E. had had the convenience of reliving those scenes and refreshing faded memories every year for more than 40 years through a unique organization.[31] Back in 1890 four teenaged boys, whom town gossips had labeled onery, shiftless, and social outcasts for whom the future held little, banded together to form the Never Sweat Club. They were L. E. Phillips, Gent A. Holland, Guy Liggett, and Archie M. Huston. The scorn they felt, sometimes even from their parents, drew them closer together than anyone could have imagined. They swore eternal friendship and adopted gold safety pins as insignias.

To cement the bond between them, they pooled their resources—two horses, a rickety old wagon, and a banged-up phonograph with two earphones—and made a tour of Western states as entrepreneurs, selling furniture polish on a farm-to-farm basis and charging a nickel to listen to two tunes on their music contraption. When they could not sell their polish for money, they bartered for chickens and fresh eggs. Following this trip they vowed to meet annually for the rest of their lives, regardless of the distance which might separate them in the future. It was a vow they kept religiously.

In the mid-nineties, the original "four horsemen" stuck together like cockleburrs and the club prospered. Then in 1897, three more "bright young sparks of Conway" became eligible (had come under the ban of village gossips) for membership: Ottway C. Zingg, L. E. Ellis, and W. H. Lake. In 1898 the Club held its annual meeting in Creston where two actions were taken: Claude Fisher was elected to membership, and the name of the organization was changed to the Anchor Club. Waite Phillips was then too young for membership; he had to wait several years before becoming the ninth and final member of the Club.

The members matured and moved in all directions, eight of them entering business, one, Ott Zingg, electing to remain in education for his career. But each year all of them made their way to a designated site where they relived the tales of their youth, played pitch for the right to possess traveling trophies, and, in general, just recharged their batteries and updated each other on what was happening in their lives. They once formed an Anchor Investment Company with a capital of $10,000, but it was more a device to weld their interests together than a scheme to make them wealthy. When interest waned, as it inevitably would, it was L. E. who urged them on to greater unity and participation in their annual meetings. Three of their number preceded L. E. in death: W. H. Lake in 1932, Ott Zingg in 1935, and Gent Holland in 1937, but all the others were present in 1943 when L. E. attended his last, the 53rd, annual meeting of the beloved Anchor Club.

The Club was a genuine reflection of L. E.'s character and personal needs. He revered his heritage and enjoyed the self-renewing qualities which his association with childhood friends brought him. He knew the value of friendship and how to be one, and he derived inspiration from the success of each of his "pals," all of whom had begun in humble settings, yet none of whom coveted the fortunes of another. In fact, the Club put friendship above all else; to them there was something greater than material wealth in their love for each other. There is an interesting, but unconfirmed story, that the members early in their club's history filled a brown jug with corn liquor and buried it in an undisclosed place in Iowa. The last surviving member was pledged to return to the secret hiding place and drink a farewell toast to all those who had passed away. Singing "The Little Brown Jug" at each annual meeting had more meaning than a mere ritual. An editorial writer summed it up in 1928 with a deft pen: "A friendship that can hold eight persons closely together for 37 years is something that must command the admiration of us all. The Anchor Club members are getting something out of life that most of us are missing in this day of rush and scramble to attain individual success and fortune."[32]

Most of the activities which occupied L. E.'s attention during his retirement years were parts of a continua which had earlier antecedents. Even his poor health seemed to have had its origins in Conway, where he often had to combat physical weakness or a constitutional susceptibility to illness. Smoking intensified his rapid heartbeat, and the tensions of a fretful, workaholic attitude increased his hypertension. When internal complications entered his life, the beginning of the end was set in motion.

By slowing his pace, and by absenting the business

32nd annual meeting of the Anchor Club, at 1201 Cherokee Street, in December, 1924.

scene, he undoubtedly prolonged his life by several years. However, a warning came in May of 1942 when he spent several days in a Kansas City hospital for treatment of a leg. The ailment had worsened in recent years. An old friend at Christmas time in 1940 had written, "Gee, it's tough to see you having to lean upon that cane, especially here at Christmas time when you and the boys make all these many nice calls . . . . Can't you figure out some way to do it and make it easier on you?"[33]

It was not in L. E.'s nature to figure out an easier way when he was performing a service or bringing Christmas cheer. But eventually he was obliged to seek medical aid for his increasing enfeeblement. He recovered somewhat; then less than a year later, L. E. suffered a stroke which partially paralyzed one-half of his body and left him unable to speak. He was deluged with telegrams, letters, and cards expressing optimism that he would defeat this latest setback the same way he had countless other temporary distresses.[34] Such was not to be the case.

One wonders what passed through Lee Eldas' mind, which remained alert and sharp through his ordeal, when he read the letter he received on August 16, 1943, from grandson Phil Starr, who lived in Kansas City. It began, "Dear Daddy Lee: I want to wish you a happy birthday, and I hope you are getting better. We go swimming every day. How hot is it in Bartlesville? It got up to a hundred yesterday."[35]

Swimming everyday! Just a few months back, he and Frank and Ed had walked by the old swimming hole where they, at Phil Starr's age, had gone swimming every day in the hot summer. His children's children had begun the cycle of growing up, much the same as Lee Eldas had done almost 60 years before. He must have drawn comfort from knowing that the cycle would be unbroken, at least for Phil's generation, and that his heritage and values had been passed along securely to another generation of Phillips-Standish heirs.

9

THE LAST YEARS

As a practicing Christian, L. E. knew his scriptures, especially the one which told him that "no man knoweth when the hour cometh" to depart this world. But he knew also from his prolonged struggle against high blood pressure and a faulty heart that the end might come at any time. As the decade of the forties began, he restricted his activities mostly to Philson Farms and only the most essential traveling. Some of his time, indeed increasing amounts of it, was spent in hospital confinement.

The war in Europe and growing economic tensions throughout the world were unsettling to him. His sons were of service age, and the future security of his family caused him much concern. He turned, in one of his moments of emotional distress, to K. S. "Boots" Adams, who recently had become President of Phillips Petroleum. "I wish I could be more optimistic," he wrote to Adams on December 26, 1940, "of the immediate and long distant future, but I cannot be. Never has the world been—at least in its economic existence—in such turmoil, and every projecting thought we may have as to the future leads us into a blind alley." As though he were placing full reliance on the young company President, he concluded, "I have full confidence that my investment and my family [are in good hands and] will be guided to a safe port."[1]

Adams was deeply moved by the tenor of L. E.'s letter. He must have sensed that Phillips was counting on him to provide help and security for his family in the event that death should overtake him. Adams' response was reassuring: he pledged to work hard to merit the confidence L. E. had expressed. "I fully realize the importance of this to you and your family, not only due to the substantial investment you have in the Company but on account of your personal interest, since you were one of the most influential factors in its development to the position it holds in the industry today."[2]

Nothing Adams could have written would have pleased L. E. more. Although he had shunned publicity, he did take immense pride in the contribution he had made as co-founder of Phillips Petroleum. It was pleasing to have others acknowledge his importance, especially one of the new generation of Phillips administrators. Perhaps it is a condition of the aging process that makes men fear they will be forgotten, but L. E. should not have overly concerned himself with such thoughts. The cobblestones he had marked over a 65-year span had gathered no moss. They shone like spotlights, lighting a path of enviable successes from Conway, Iowa, to Bartlesville, Oklahoma. At this point in his life, he simply had to walk down the path more slowly, though from early outward signs, the slowing was hardly noticeable.

January 12, 1941, found L. E. and Node in Los Angeles with several other residents of Bartlesville and Tulsa for the wedding of Waite's son, Elliott, to Miss Barbara Riley. On the same day in Bartlesville, he was appointed chairman of the committee on agriculture for the Chamber of Commerce. His life of community service was continuing, no doubt in this case owing to his long-time interest in his own farm and to his persistent encouragement of 4-H Club and vocational agriculture activities. In fact, Philson Farms had become "the Mecca of the livestock-minded youth of Oklahoma."[3]

The farm was a beautiful, restful place. L. E. and his son, Phil, had stocked the sprawling 700-acre spread

Phillips enjoyed a good ruse, especially when extolling the achievements of his farm. In this "doctored" photograph, L.E. would have you think his chickens grew to mammoth sizes.

with the finest specimens of various breeds obtainable, but their "pride and joy" was a small but select herd of Poland China hogs. Philson boasted the most modern facilities, and Earl Potter, superintendent of the farm, kept the grounds in show-place condition. With an "innate love of the soil and an inherent liking for animal life"—and a pressing need to relax—L. E. found great joy and comfort from his frequent trips to the farm.[4]

His agricultural interests provided a needed but controlled outlet for his pent-up energies. He accepted a three-year appointment to the Washington County Fair Board, and set out to promote the fair. He told an overflow crowd at the annual Dewey Chamber of Commerce dinner that they should not be "town conscious but county conscious"; they should "put their shoulders to the wheel and make a success" of the fair. He then distributed 18 calves to 4-H Club members in the county, 17 of them on a deferred plan which allowed the boys to pay for their calves after they had been fattened, shown, and sold at the county fair. And he spent his personal money improving the fair grounds, pledging an impressive list of cash prizes in a variety of competitive categories for both men and women. L. E. was not known for doing things halfway.[5]

Little wonder that Washington Countians began to expect the biggest fair in history. Phillips was delighted, not only because a record 4000 people jammed the fairgrounds on September 9, 1941, but also because Philson Farms' Poland China hogs and White-faced Hereford cattle won numerous ribbons.[6]

Apparently the pressure was too much for the frail L. E. He took a few days vacation before and after the opening of the fair. In August he relaxed in San Francisco, but even then he could not escape the press. He was asked about the war in Europe, and with typical optimism he responded, "This war will be won by oil and the brains directing its use." He further indicated that Phillips Petroleum was a leader in developing synthetic rubber. Following that trip, he then joined two of his brothers, Frank and Ed, on September 19 for what was to prove to be a last return trip to his boyhood home in Conway, Iowa. The nostalgic visit did wonders for his spirits, but the exertion again took its toll on his energy.[7]

L. E. was in St. Luke's Hospital in Kansas City when Pearl Harbor was attacked on December 7, 1941. The pattern was becoming familiar: a few weeks of activity followed by a few days of recuperation. For instance, he was present at the 28th Annual Meeting of the Past Presidents of the OBA on May 7, 1942, but was unable to attend the May 26 Bartlesville Chamber of Commerce Banquet which honored Frank Phillips on the Silver Anniversary of the founding of Phillips Petroleum Company. It was a major civic event, and L. E.'s absence was

Frank presents L.E. with a watch, a gift each employee received for 25 years of service to the company.

sorely felt by the large crowd. However, a grateful Frank paid tribute to his ailing brother who was "under treatment" in a hospital, a gesture which was greeted with approval by the vast audience.[8]

Providence did permit L. E. to attend a special recognition banquet honoring those employees who had accumulated 25 years of continuous service with Phillips. The ceremony, held at Frank's Woolaroc retreat, recognized and awarded Hamilton watches to 11 men who had been with the company since its incorporation on

25th Anniversary of the Phillips Petroleum Company, held at Woolaroc on June 13, 1942, to honor those with 25 years of service to the company.

June 13, 1917. Honored also were 12 men and one woman with 25 years of recognized service, a part of which had been earned in companies merged or purchased by Phillips Petroleum Company.[9]

It was an occasion for reflection. For a company which in 1927 was still a producer of crude oil and natural gas, Phillips in 1942 held an impressive number of "firsts" in the industry: the largest producer of natural gasoline in the world; the largest marketer of liquified petroleum gases and related products; the largest supplier of gas for the manufacture of carbon black; and the first company to develop gasoline matched to seasonal conditions. Additionally, Phillips was among the few major companies which consistently produced more crude oil than its refinery requirements; it was among the leaders in petroleum research, among the largest producers of natural gas, and held one of the strongest patent positions in the industry. After 25 years, Phillips

Petroleum stood "proudly as a momument to the American way."[10]

About the anniversary observance, a columnist for the *Bartlesville Morning Examiner* wrote: "What a lot of water has gone over the dam since Frank and L. E. Phillips founded the Phillips Petroleum Company 25 years ago. These men had a lot of fun out of what they have done, but we doubt if they would like to do it over again. That is the beauty about life. Once is enough to live it."[11]

Both L. E. and Frank had enjoyed their years as oilmen, and they prided themselves on being able to remember and name participants in events which happened more than 50 years before. Perhaps it was because they did remember and showed their appreciation that employees of the Phillips Petroleum Company revered them so highly.[12]

Hardly had the observance passed than the war touched L. E. directly. On July 31, 1942, Philip Rex took the oath of office and was commissioned a lieutenant, senior grade, in the United States Navy Reserve. The same rank was awarded John W. Starr, Martha Jane's husband. Both were sent to training schools to prepare for permanent assignments in the Navy. Lee, Jr., was not called to service. And, as if the anxiety of having the boys on active duty was not enough, there was a measurable amount of resentment toward the few Japanese in Bartlesville, a fact which forced L. E. to send his longtime trusty worker and chauffeur, Harry, to live at Philson Farms for the duration. The war was disrupting the tranquility of Lee Eldas' home life.[13]

Fortunately, the annual meeting of the Anchor Club, the 52nd, provided some diversion. Time had altered many things, but relaxing with old friends at Excelsior Springs, Missouri, in October was a tonic. The *Kansas City Star* made much of the fact that "milk was the main item on the menu." L. E. explained, "There were days

The last meeting of the Anchor Club which L.E. attended. The dinner was held at 1201 Cherokee Street, but L.E., seated at the head of the table, retired early because of his illness.

when it was champagne, but years make a lot of changes in your outlook and your stomach."[14] The years, however, had not changed their desire to "swap the same old yarns" or to check to see if each member wore the required gold anchor in his lapel and carried a buckeye in his pocket. They still assessed a fine of $5 which went into the Club treasury if either was missing. It was to be the last meeting L. E. could truly enjoy, although he would meet one more time with his cherished boyhood friends.

Over the next few months, Lee Eldas' external activities were restricted to supporting roles. He opened his home at Christmas time, along with other Bartlesville residents, to servicemen at nearby Army and Navy bases. He hosted the York Rite annual picnic at Philson, standing in for Phil who was on Navy duty. And he assisted Waite in a Red Cross War Fund drive. But mostly he spent his time "puttering around his farm" where Clyde

Reasor, agriculture feature writer for the country newspaper, interviewed him during the last week of May.
Within a month, L. E. suffered the first of two strokes
he would have during the hot summer days of 1943.[15]

A simple news release announced the first attack,
which was adjudged "not to be serious." "A heart spe-
cialist was flown from Kansas City . . . to treat L. E.
Phillips," the article read.[16] The physician, Dr. Lindsey
Milne, had treated him many times before. Friends knew
that L. E. had been in ill health for many years, and
Milne's quick flight in a borrowed plane generated much
concern. In truth the attack of June 28 was classified as
a mini-stroke, and the most serious after-effect was a
partial but restricting loss of sight.

Then less than two months later, while he was being
driven with Node to Philson Farms by his secretary, Miss
Dorothy Saunders, he suffered a second and far more
damaging stroke which affected the right side of his
body and robbed him of his speech.[17] Additionally, he
had some difficulty in coordinating his thoughts when
he tried to talk, which was a problem since he could not
do so. However, he could communicate reasonably well
through a type of sign language and quite well by writing
out what he wished done.

When the second attack came, he was rushed back
to 1201 Cherokee where Dr. H. C. Weber was called to
attend him. A strange phenomenon occured. Philip Rex,
miles away at a Navy Gunnery School near Purcell, had
a premonition that something was wrong and called to
ask if his father was all right. He was told by Dr. Weber,
who answered the telephone, that his father was gravely
ill.[18]

For Node and the children, who came to visit their
father frequently in the months that followed, there
began a lonely vigil as they watched a former workaholic
struggle against his enervating confinement. Miss Saunders continued to work with him on business-related

L.E. and Node with children and grandchildren at Christmas time, 1939.

matters, and he was attended by Miss Annie Garrow, a strong-willed nurse whom he had met during his several trips to the Thornton-Minor Clinic in Kansas City. Node ran the household and provided companionship during long conversationless hours.

Node was a lovely woman, frail herself but always the devoted wife. The crisis months were not burdening because she felt deeply about L. E. She could remember the supportive, poetic telegram she received from him on her birthday on April 28, 1915, while she herself convalesced in Denver: "So brief our existence," he wired her. "A glimpse at the most is all we can have of those we hold dear, and oft even joy is unheeded and lost for want of your heart who could echo it."[19] And she could recall the flowers on her anniversary and a special card which read: "You are a very patient and sweet woman to have stood by me 39 years."[20] The ensuing months were painful only because she knew instinctively that her husband's condition was irreversible.

Occasionally, L. E. was a problem for others. Miss Saunders could anticipate most of his instructions and interpret his mumblings. Infrequently, he became short tempered and at least once she left the house because of an irritable attitude. But a patient Node urged him to apologize, which he did. And Annie, who had a way with L. E., managed his medical needs and chastised him for his smoking, claiming he would one day burn his lovely house down. When he gestured in his sign language that it was his house and he would burn it down if he wished, Annie's typical response was, "Well, let me get out of it before you start!"[21]

L. E. received numerous messages of encouragement and visits from old friends, such as Alf Landon. As the time approached for the 53rd annual meeting of the Anchor Club, he urged his friends to meet in Bartlesville because it was unlikely that he could join them in another location. They agreed, knowing that it might well be their last meeting with him. It would prove to be.[22]

The other four surviving members, Guy Liggett, L. E. Ellis, Archie Huston, and Claude Fisher, met first at Frank's house on October 8, 1943, then paid a brief visit to Lee's home just to check on him. They headquartered at Woolaroc where Frank sat in for L. E. in the annual pitch contest and won for him the right to keep the traveling trophy for the coming year. A sort of last supper was staged at L. E.'s home on Saturday evening, an old-fashioned country dinner with large pitchers of milk. The occasion was recorded on film, and the snapshots revealed a pale, thin Lee Eldas Phillips. When they departed for their homes, the other members realized the Anchor Club would never be the same again, for it must have been obvious to them that L. E. would not survive for long.[23]

For a time after the Club meeting, L. E. seemed to improve in health and regained a halting part of his speech. But an old asthmatic condition worsened. Nurses administered increasing amounts of medication, but his breathing was labored. Given his high blood pressure and recurring stomach problems, it is remarkable that he did not suffer more.[24] He died quietly on Sunday, April 16, 1944, at 10:00 a.m. All the children were at home at the time, a comforting support to a saddened Node.[25]

The flood of messages of condolence was almost overwhelming. Telegrams, cards, and letters poured in to Bartlesville.[26] News releases recounted his career and hailed his successes. Stories long forgotten resurfaced in the wake of one so highly esteemed. He was, as one release detailed, a one-time corn husking champion of Iowa, having in 1890 husked 110 bushels in eight hours.[27] Another told of the offer General Patrick Hurley had made to him during the Hoover administration to become governor-general of the Philippines.[28] Yet another recalled the story about a young man who was being fired from Phillips because he had struck a match with almost disasterous results while cleaning an oil tank. When every member of the executive staff except Lee Eldas voted to discharge him, Frank asked him to explain his vote. "Well," L. E. reasoned, "if we keep him, we will know that we will have at least one man working for us who will never strike a match in the wrong place."[29] The employee was retained.

Eulogies sprang from a variety of sources. Clyde Reasor of the *Washington Countian* wrote affectionately that "Mr. Phillips meant more to Bartlesville and Washington County . . . than probably the average citizen realized." He added, "His counsel was in demand at all times by different organizations, and he was always working for the best interest" of his city, county, and state.[30] A *Tulsa World* editorial noted that "he was never conspicuous and he was not as well known as others in the industry, but he was potent all the same."[31] A Kansas newspaper editorialized that "Lee Phillips' life shows what opportunities young Americans have," adding, "the benefit to the world of such men as the Phillips brothers is very great."[32]

The *Bartlesville Daily Enterprise* mourned his passing. "Bartlesville lost another of the men who helped make a sprawling, brawling oil village into one of the best . . . smaller cities in the United States when Lee Eldas Phillips died Sunday. But Bartians lost more than that. They lost a friend, a neighbor, and an outstanding father. Those qualities . . . transcend any and all of L. E.'s material accomplishments and the national prominence he attained. Big men, after all, are figuratively, a dime a dozen in this great land. Real friends, real neighbors, and real fathers aren't . . . . L. E. Phillips leaves a memory that money couldn't buy and that fame along couldn't possibly have created."[33]

Friends echoed the sentiment. Amon Carter wired Node, "I was shocked this morning to hear of the death of sweet old L. E. Bless his heart, all of his friends will miss him. He was a sweet character with a great sense of humor and I have never known anyone I enjoyed being with more . . . ."[34] One of his nurses, Victoria McDougal Heller, telegraphed, "It was a privilege to share—in knowing him and serving too—he wasn't just a patient; he was the kindest man I ever knew."[35]

Funeral services were held on Tuesday afternoon at the First Christian Church in Bartlesville with, among others, his old friend and former pastor, the Reverend Harry Ice, officiating. In a beautifully sensitive message depicting L. E.'s most memorable qualities, Reverend Ice concluded, "L. E., thou are gone from this life but not soon will thy many admiring friends and adoring loved ones forget the blessings thou hast bequeathed upon us." Interment was in Memorial Park in Bartlesville.[36]

It took some time for the volume of mournful expressions to decline. Such remembrances were consoling to Node and her children—and would have pleased had L. E. had the privilege to hear them. He once had written that his "philosophy of life is that if I am entitled to any bouquets, I prefer to have them while I live, and I think that kind words and smiles to the living are of far more value than tons of flowers on our bier."[37] To be remembered so affectionately and respectfully meant that he would live on in the hearts and memories of those whom he had befriended and loved.

The passing of Lee Eldas Phillips marked another cobblestone on the road he had traveled for more than 67 years, but it was far from the last to be labeled. As long as there are new goals announced and accomplishments realized by the company he helped co-found, his name, along with brother Frank's, rightfully should be on each new stone of achievement as reminders of their courageous efforts and unselfish sacrifices to which all generations of Phillips executives and employees will be forever indebted.

L. E. Phillips was a man deserving of every accolade and recognition which can be given him. Rising from the veritable rags in the Iowa corn patches to the enviable riches of the Oklahoma oil fields, he left an example of rugged individualism and personal triumph seldom equaled in American business heritage. The Rockefellers, Carnegies, and Morgans were moguls of an earlier era upon whom scorn has been heaped because of their insensitive business dealings with their competitors. The Phillips brothers—Frank, L. E., and Waite—rose in a different business era to heights equal to most of the earlier titans without the accompanying onus of unfair competitive practices. The Phillips brothers truly were talented players who successfully competed in the big leagues with Eastern professionals, never once paying homage to or showing disrespect for

184 / L. E. PHILLIPS

them. And L. E.'s contributions to the company—his stability, his good business judgment, his loyalty and willingness to work hard, and his penchant for organization and good personal relations—even today are incalculable.

Oklahomans young and old have a model by which to measure their own contributions to the quality of life which they enjoy, for L. E. Phillips gave liberally of his time and talents to a wide range of civic, professional, and social causes. He did so with an unassuming flair, most of the time without seeking recognition and never to be remunerated. It was his way of returning to the people of Bartlesville, Oklahoma, and the nation some of the blessings he had been permitted to experience.

If one cobblestone shines brighter than the others he marked during his rich, full life, it would be the one labeled character—the honest devotion he had to the most meaningful aspects of his life: his family, his country, the American private enterprise system, and his commitment to make his world better for all to share.

Lee Eldas Phillips loved Tennyson's "Thanatopsis" and lived his life in such a fashion that when his summons came "to enter the silent halls of death," he did so with dignity and the universal respect of his contemporaries. As the old saying goes, "None knew him but to love him."

NOTES

Chapter 1

¹L. E. Phillips to Mike Cotter, April 4, 1905. Phillips disciplined himself from early life to collect and assemble numerous materials: scrapbooks, photograph albums, autobiographical notes, and genealogies. The letter cited was returned to L. E. by Cotter on July 2, 1937, with the note, "At least I knew you WHEN. And here is the goods [letter] to prove it." The letter was placed in one of the many scrapbooks which are in the possession of his eldest son, Philip Rex Phillips, of Bartlesville, Oklahoma. All of these materials hereinafter are cited as the *LEP Collection*.

²Autobiographical Notes, *LEP Collection*. The eight pages of these notes cover only the recollections of his youth in Iowa and his early years in Bartlesville. According to Philip R. Phillips, the family urged him repeatedly during his retirement years to complete his reminiscences, but to no avail.

³"If We Hadn't Hit the Anna, We'd Have Been Back in Iowa," *Shield* (Phillips Petroleum Company), IV, No. 4 (1979), 3-5; Autobiographical Notes, *LEP Collection*.

⁴Genealogy, Phillips Family; genealogy, "Life of Mary Jane Tate [Fawcett]"; *LEP Collection*.

⁵Genealogy, Standish Family; genealogy, Phillips Family; *LEP Collection*.

⁶Genealogy, "Family Record of Matthew Kettle Standish and Esther Curtis Standish," *LEP Collection*. The record includes brief accounts of Daniel Phillips and his son, Lewis Franklin Phillips.

⁷Genealogy, "Lineage of Thomas Linch Fawcett," *LEP Collection*.

⁸Genealogy, Family Record of Matthew Kettle Standish and Esther Curtis Standish," *LEP Collection*.

⁹Autobiographical Notes, *LEP Collection*. *Philnews* (Special Edition), November 28, 1939, p. 8.

¹⁰*Gravity* (Iowa) *Republican*, July 5, 1917; interview, Philip Rex Phillips with author, July, 1980, tape in Oklahoma Heritage Association Archives, Oklahoma City. All interviews obtained for this biography are held by the Oklahoma Heritage Association Archives, hereinafter referred to as *OHAA*. Born Lee Eldas Phillips according to an old family Bible entry, L. E. throughout his life erroneously was referred to as Lee Elda, especially in the press.

¹¹Autobiographical Notes, *LEP Collection*. The balance of the

material in this chapter, unless otherwise noted, is drawn from L. E. Phillips' Autobiographical Notes.

[12]*Oklahoma Banker*, February 1914, p. 7.

[13]Photograph Albums, annotated by L. E. Phillips, *LEP Collection*.

[14]J. M. Hussey, "To Whom It May Concern," November 13, 1894; William G. Bishop, "To Whom This May Come," October 11, 1895, *LEP Collection*. Hussey described "Elda Phillips" as a very industrious and painstaking young man in every thing." Bishop stated that he would "take pleasure in recommending him to any who may desire the services of a competent clerk or accountant."

[15]Autobiographical Notes, *LEP Collection*. *The Anchor Club* (Photograph Album), *LEP Collection*.

[16]*The Midwestern* (Des Moines, Iowa), February, 1910. p. 10.

Chapter 2

[1]*Omaha Evening World*, December 11, 1925; Autobiographical Notes, *LEP Collection*.

[2]Autobiographical Notes. *LEP Collection*. Again the narrative portions of this chapter, though frequently enriched by the references cited hereafter, are drawn from Phillips' Autobiographical Notes.

[3]Photograph Albums, annotated by LEP, *LEP Collection*.

[4]Lock Campbell, "To Whom It May Concern," November 23, 1897. The letter stated in part, "L. E. Phillips taught the fall term in our district and has afforded us perfect satisfaction. We can cheerfully recommend him to any board of directors to whom he may apply."

[5]Phillips made and kept a photograph of this group of students. The description he left in his Autobiographical Notes certainly is verified by the picture and implicitly attests to his courage.

[6]*Conway Journal*, June 24, 1898.

[7]*Conway Journal*, November 28, 1898; Unidentified newsclipping, *LEP Collection*.

[8]*Creston Morning American*, March 27, 1899; Photograph Album, annotated by LEP, *LEP Collection*. Pictures of his first office building and of Ed Bowden are included.

[9]Photograph Albums, *LEP Collection*. Pictures of Rex and the new office location in Creston are included with identifying annotations.

[10]This was the most dramatic episode Phillips described in his Autobiographical notes.

[11]*Creston Daily Examiner*, November 13, 1902; *Creston Daily Advertiser*, November 14, 1902.

[12]Unidentified newsclipping, *LEP Collection*.

[13]*Conway Journal*, October 9, 1901.

[14]Apparently Phillips attended the recital; a copy of the program for that evening was included in an early scrapbook, *LEP Collection*.

[15]Photograph Album, annotated by LEP, *LEP Collection*.

[16]*Creston Daily Advertiser*, November 26, 1902; *The Advertiser* listed the Reverend T. L. Fawcett of Conway, "grandfather of the groom," as performing the official ceremony.

[17]*Creston Morning American*, November 29, 1902.

[18]This data is drawn from annotations Phillips made to identify several pictures in one of the early Photograph Albums, *LEP Collection*.

[19]*Creston Daily Advertiser*, November 14, 1902.

[20]The officers were reelected at the "annual meeting" of the stockholders in April. The company was described as "the best if not the largest in Marion County." *Creston Daily Advertiser*, April 12, 1903.

[21]There are several unidentified clippings from Iowa newspapers in the *LEP Collection* which tell briefly of Phillips' business travels during 1903-04. One lengthy article details his and Myers' experiences at the Des Moines meeting.

[22]"If We Hadn't Hit With the Anna, We'd Have Been Back in Iowa," *Shield*, IV, No. 4 (1979), 3-5. This account is written from Phillips' Autobiographical Notes, *LEP Collection*.

[23]The items unfortunately are undated and unidentified, *LEP Collection*.

Chapter 3

[1]These are the descriptive words Phillips used in his Autobiographical Notes, *LEP Collection*. Pictures made of the bustling oil town at the turn of the century confirm his observations. See for example: Joe Williams, *Bartlesville: Remembrances of Times Past, Reflections of Today* (Bartlesville: TRW Reda Pump Division, 1979), pp. 34-35; *Philnews* (Special Edition), November 28, 1939, p. 8; Washington County Historical Society, *A Pictorial History of Bartlesville* (Bartlesville: Washington County Historical Society, Inc., 1972), p. 46.

[2]Autobiographical Notes, *LEP Collection*; Williams, *Bartlesville*, p. 88.

[3]Williams, *Bartlesville*, p. 109.

[4]*Knoxville* (Iowa) *Journal*, June 5, 1905; Autobiographical Notes, *LEP Collection*.

[5]"If We Hadn't Hit With the Anna, We'd Have Been Back in Iowa," *Shield*, IV, No. 4 (1979), 4.

[6]*Ibid.*

[7]"Anna Anderson Davis," *Shield*, IV, No. 4 (1979), 6.

[8]Williams, *Bartlesville*, p. 109; *Tulsa Daily World*, January 28, 29, 30, 1964.

[9]*Bartlesville Morning Examiner*, December 4, 1905.

[10]Autobiographical Notes, *LEP Collection*.

[11]*Ibid.*

[12]*Bartlesville Daily Enterprise*, September 24, 1908. The check noted

is in the *LEP Collection* and shows a discrepancy between the numerical and written amounts. The numerical amount was $800 and the check is marked "paid," Phillips was too good a banker to have paid himself more than the written value of $80.

[13]Autobiographical Notes, *LEP Collection.*

[14]Interview, Philip Rex Phillips with author, July 10, 1980, *OHAA.*

[15]*Bartlesville Daily Enterprise*, July 8, 1908; *Bartlesville Morning Examiner*, July 8, 1908.

[16]*Bartlesville Daily Enterprise*, August 1, 1908.

[17]*Bartlesville Morning Examiner*, November 10, 1908, December 5, 1908; unidentified newspaper advertisement, *LEP Collection.*

[18]*Bartlesville Daily Enterprise*, November 7, 1908; *Bartlesville Morning Examiner*, November 7, 10, 1908.

[19]*Bartlesville Daily Enterprise*, November 11, 1908; the *Independence Reporter* article was carried in the *Bartlesville Morning Examiner*, November 12, 1908.

[20]Autobiographical Notes, *LEP Collection.*

[21]*Southwestern Banker*, October, 1914; *Oklahoma Banker*, April, 1911, p. 10. *Commercial West*, July 11, 1914; *North Dakota Banker*, January, 1918, pp. 31-38.

[22]*New State Tribune*, April 27, 1911.

[23]*Bartlesville Daily Enterprise*, April 1, 1911; *Bartlesville Morning Examiner*, April 2, 1911. The condensed statements for December 5, 1911, and September 4, 1912, were official Bank publications, *LEP Collection.* The *Bank News* issued was "Vol. 1, No. 1" as cited in an undated newsclipping, *LEP Collection.*

[24]Autobiographical Notes, *LEP Collection.*

[25]Unidentified newsclipping, *LEP Collection.*

[26]L. E. Phillips, "Our Taxation System," *Oklahoma Banker*, April, 1911, pp. 8-10.

[27]*Oklahoma Banker*, June, 1915, p. 11; *Daily Oklahoman*, May 18, 1916; *Bartlesville Morning Examiner*, May 18, 1916; *Western Financier*, May, 1916, p. 40; James M. Smallwood, *An Oklahoma Adventure: Of Banks and Bankers* (Norman: Oklahoma Heritage Association, 1979), pp. 205; 207.

[28]*Bartlesville Morning Examiner*, May 18, 1916.

[29]*Ibid.* May 13, 1916; *Kansas City Journal*, September 25, 29, 1916; *Bartlesville Morning Examiner*, September 26, 1916; *Western Financier*, September, 1916, p. 1.

[30]William Howard Taft to L. E. Phillips, telegram dated April 13, 1917; Paul Malone to L. E. Phillips, letter dated April 13, 1917.

[31]Williams, *Bartlesville*, pp. 109-112; *Oklahoma Banker*, March, 1919, pp. 9-10.

[32]*Oklahoma Banker*, March, 1919, pp. 9-10.

[33]*Bartlesville Daily Enterprise*, April 30, 1920; *Bartlesville Morning Examiner*, May 1, 1920.

[34]*Coast Banker*, November, 1921, p. 18; *Oklahoma Banker*, November, 1917, p. 5.

[35]*Bartlesville Morning Examiner*, April 15, 18, 22, 28, 1914; *Bartlesville Daily Enterprise*, April 23, 1914; *Daily Oklahoman*, April 20, 1914; *Kansas City Post*, May 2, 1914.

[36]*Bartlesville Morning Examiner*, June 3, 1914; *Bartlesville Daily Enterprise*, June 3, 1914.

[37]*Kansas City Star*, December 7, 1926; *Bartlesville Morning Examiner*, December 7, 1926; *Oklahoma Banker*, December, 1926, p. 5.

[38]M. L. McClure (Chairman of Board, Federal Reserve Bank of Kansas City) to L. E. Phillips, letter dated February 8, 1930.

Chapter 4

[1]Handwritten note by L. E. Phillips, *LEP Collection. Bartlesville Daily Enterprise*, November 30, 1910.

[2]Interview, Ms. Dorothy Saunders with author, July 28, 1980, *OHAA*. Ms. Saunders served as secretary to both Mr. and Mrs. L. E. Phillips and later to Philip Rex Phillips.

[3]Interview, Philip Rex Phillips with author, July 20, 1980, *OHAA*. The framework for much of this chapter was obtained through interviews and personal discussions with Philip R. Phillips.

[4]Pictures of the home are contained in the Photograph Albums, *LEP Collections*.

[5]*Bartlesville Morning Examiner*, September 21, 22, 1909.

[6]*Ibid*. August 27, 1908. *Bartlesville Daily Enterprise*, November 12, 1912.

[7]See for example, *Bartlesville Morning Examiner*, July 13, 14, 30, 1909; September 15, 1909; *Bartlesville Daily Enterprise*, July 7, 9, 15, 25, 28, 1910. L. E. Phillips was depicted in one article as being so lonely during his family's stay in Colorado that he went to Frank's house one Saturday and "almost wore out a phonograph record" which reminded him of his daughter, Martha Jane. *Bartlesville Daily Enterprise*, August 28, 1910. In another, he rejoiced at learning that doctors told Node she could finally leave Denver and return to Bartlesville. *Oklahoma Banker*, September, 1915. p. 10.

[8]Interview, Philip Rex Phillips with author, July 10, 1980. *OHAA*.

[9]*Bartlesville Morning Examiner*, December 8, 1921; May 6, 1922; July 3, 1921; February 17, 1922; *The Nautilus* (Bartlesville High School), March 21, 1923; October 10, 1924.

[10]*Bartlesville Morning Examiner*, May 21, 1922; Bartlesville High School, Graduation Program, May 25, 1922, *LEP Collection*; *Bartlesville Morning Examiner*, June 1, 1926.

[11]Bartlesville High School, Graduation Program, May 17, 1928, *LEP Collection*; *Bartlesville Morning Examiner*, January 26, 1923; February 5, 1928.

[12]*Bartlesville Morning Examiner*, May 31, 1925; Bartlesville High School, Graduation Program, May 27, 1925, *LEP Collection; Bartlesville Morning Examiner*, September 2, 1925.

[13]See for example, *Bartlesville Morning Examiner*, December 30, 1924; May 25, 1925; September 12, 1925.

[14]Interview, Philip Rex Phillips with author, July 10, 1980, *OHAA*.

[15]Interview, Ms. Dorothy Saunders with author, July 28, 1980, *OHAA*; Dorothy Saunders to Billy M. Jones, letter dated July 30, 1980, *OHAA*.

[16]The telegrams were sent from Amarillo and Vernon, Texas, to Mrs. Phillips at the Muehlbach Hotel in Kansas City, *LEP Collection*.

[17]Ms. Dorothy Saunders to Billy M. Jones, July 30, 1980. Ms. Saunders generously sent the author a postscript to her interview of July 28, 1980, adding a few excellent anecdotes which she had overlooked.

[18]*Bartlesville Daily Enterprise*, undated newsclipping, *LEP Collection; Oklahoma City Times*, November 4, 1931.

[19]*Bartlesville Morning Examiner*, May 30, 1926; Programme Musicale, June 10, 1926, *LEP Collection*. A lengthy news item telling of the 'outstanding musicale in the Phillips' home' attested to the popular reception of both the instrument and the program. "Imported artists" for the occasion were George B. Kemp, Jr., organist; Mrs. Helen Cahoon, Coloratura soprano, both from Chicago, and Mrs. Robert Graver, accompanist, of Kansas City. Miss Bernice Breazeale of Bartlesville arranged the program and performed as violinist. *Bartlesville Morning Examiner*, June 11, 1926.

[20]Lawrence E. Smith, "Oil Company Executive is Elected to Federal Reserve Board," *National Petroleum News*, December 1, 1926, p. 8.

[21]Interview, Paul Endacott with author, July 28, 1980, *OHAA*. Interview, L. E. Fitzgarrald with author, September 29, 1980, *OHAA*. Interview, Glenroy Billbe with author, September 29, 1980, *OHAA*; Interview, Philip Rex Phillips with author, July 10, 1980, *OHAA*. "Phillips 'Pete' Adventures in Chemistry," *Business Week*, December 31, 1949, pp. 22-24.

[22]Interview, Philip Rex Phillips with author, July 10, 1980.

[23]*Ibid.*

[24]*Bulletin* (University of Tulsa), 36, No. 7 (July, 1929), 7, *LEP Collection*.

[25]Unidentified newsclipping, *LEP Collection*.

[26]*Bartlesville Daily Enterprise*, June 17, 1908.

[27]Ms. Dorothy Saunders to Billy M. Jones, July 30, 1980.

[28]The photographs are thoughtfully arranged and liberally annotated in the Photograph Albums, *LEP Collection*.

[29]*Bartlesville Morning Examiner*, January 17, 1928; interview, Philip Rex Phillips with author, July 10, 1980.

[30]*Christian Echo* (First Christian Church, Bartlesville), December 9, 1926; a new vestibule which Phillips donated, cost $12,000. *LEP Collection. Bartlesville Morning Examiner*, January 25, 1925.

[31]See for example: Rev. Harry L. Ice to L. E. Phillips, letter dated January 2, 1925, *LEP Collection; Christian Echo*, December 9, 1926.

³²See for example: *Bartlesville Morning Examiner*, May 11, 1923, *Tulsa Tribune*, November 18, 1923; *Bartlesville Daily Enterprise*, July 29, 1929.

³³Phillips infrequently reflected privately about the rejected appointment with his wife who always responded that his health, which forced his retirement from Phillips Petroleum Company, would have been no better in the Philippines. Interview, Ms Dorothy Saunders with author, July 28, 1980, *OHAA*. Interview, Philip Rex Phillips with author, July 10, 1980, *OHAA*.

³⁴Interview, Ms. Dorothy Saunders with author, July 28, 1980, *OHAA*. *Bartlesville Morning Examiner*, October 13, 1912.

³⁵Nobe Welty to L. E. Phillips, December 24, 1928. *LEP Collection*. The Weltys owned and published the *Bartlesville Morning Examiner*.

³⁶H. H. McClintock to L. E. Phillips, December 25, 1925, *LEP Collection*.

³⁷*Ibid.*

³⁸Interview, Philip Rex Phillips with author, July 10, 1980.

³⁹*Wichita Beacon*, August 11, 13, 1929; *Wichita Eagle*, August 11, 13, 1929; *Tulsa Tribune*, August 16, 1929.

⁴⁰*Bartlesville Morning Examiner*, August 16, 1929; *Bartlesville Daily Enterprise*, August 16, 1929; *Kansas City Star*, November 3, 1929; *Denver Post*, January 5, 1930.

⁴¹Martha Jane's wedding was covered in the following: *Kansas City Star*, October 27, 29, 1929, November 3, 1929; *Bartlesville Daily Enterprise*, October 26, 29, 1929; *Tulsa Daily World*, October 27, 1929; *Daily Oklahoman*, October 27, 1929; *Bartlesville Morning Examiner*, October 26, 1929; *Wichita Eagle*, November 10, 1929. L. E., Jr.'s wedding was presented in: *Wichita Eagle*, November 22, 26, 27, 1929; *Wichita Beacon*, November 24, 26, 27, 1929; *Rocky Mountain News*, October 28, 1929; *Bartlesville Daily Enterprise*, November 27, 1929; *Bartlesville Morning Examiner*, November 27, 1929; *Tulsa Tribune*, November 26, 1929.

⁴²Martha Jane Phillips Starr to Mrs. L. E. Phillips, telegram sent from Havana, Cuba, dated November 11, 1929, *LEP Collection; Wichita Eagle*, November 27, 1929; *Bartlesville Morning Examiner*, November 27, 1929.

Chapter 5

¹*Tulsa Daily World*, February 28, 1919.

²See for example, *Tulsa Daily World*, January 21, 1924.

³Interview, Paul Endacott with author, July 28, 1980, *OHAA*. Endacott provided a valuable overview for the early oil industry, having been involved continuously with Phillips Petroleum following his graduation from the University of Kansas as an engineer. He presently lives in Bartlesville.

⁴*Bartlesville Morning Examiner*, September 1, 1917.

[5]*Oklahoma Banker*, March, 1919. p. 10; *Bartlesville Morning Examiner*, May 20, 1919.

[6]Interview, L. E. Fitzgarrald with author, September 29, 1980, *OHAA*. "Fitz" began his career with Phillips Petroleum in 1919 in the Production Division. He brought to the company an organized material and equipment management system which quickly brought him respect and promotion. He retired from Phillips in 1962 and presently lives in Bartlesville; Williams, *Bartlesville*, p. 102; for a good early description of the riotous bidding wars, see *Bartlesville Daily Enterprise*, February 4, 1920.

[7]*Bartlesville Daily Enterprise*, February 4, 1920; April 15, 1920.

[8]*Bartlesville Morning Examiner*, April 5, 1921; December 13, 1921.

[9]*Ibid*. December 13, 1921; unidentified newsclipping, *LEP Collection*.

[10]*Boston Commercial*, November 26, 1921; *Tulsa Tribune*, November 29, 1921.

[11]*Tulsa Daily World*, June 28, 1921; August 22, 1921.

[12]*Ibid*, August 22, 1921.

[13]Unidentified newsclipping, *LEP Collection*.

[14]Waite Phillips to L. E. Phillips, undated telegram, *LEP Collection*. The telegram was addressed to Phillips at the Manoa Hotel, Honolulu, where L. E. and his family were vacationing.

[15]*Bartlesville Morning Examiner*, March 3, 4, 1922.

[16]*Pawhuska Daily Capital*, June 28, 1922; *Kansas City Times*, June 29, 1922.

[17]"Two Tracts Break Previous Record for Osage County Acreage," *National Petroleum News*, March 8, 1922, p. 25; *Oil and Gas Journal*, March 3, 1922; *Oklahoma City Times*, March 3, 1922.

[18]*Bartlesville Morning Examiner*, May 20, 1922; *Daily Oklahoman*, October 10, 1922.

[19]*Bartlesville Daily Enterprise*, September 17, 1922.

[20]*Bartlesville Morning Examiner*, December 17, 1922; *Philnews* (Special Edition) November 28, 1939, p. 19.

[21]See for example: *Oil and Gas Journal*, October 4, 1922, p. R-6.

[22]*Daily Oklahoman*, October 10, 1922; unidentified newsclipping, *LEP Collection*.

[23]*Bartlesville Morning Examiner*, May 20, 1922.

[24]Williams, *Bartlesville*, p. 120; *Philnews* (Special Edition), November 28, 1939; *Shield* (20th Anniversary Edition), June, 1937, p. 30; interview, Philip Rex Phillips with author, July 10, 1980, *OHAA*.

[25]Kenny Franks, *The Oklahoma Petroleum Industry* (Norman: University of Oklahoma Press, 1980), pp. 37-39.

[26]*Ibid*.; Harold F. Williamson and others, *The American Petroleum Industry*, 2 vols. (Evanston: Northwestern University Press, 1959, 1963), II, 421-422.

[27]Interview, Paul Endacott with author, July 28, 1980, *OHAA*; *Shield*, June, 1937, pp. 22-23.

[28]*Bartlesville Morning Examiner*, April 5, 1923.

[29]*Kansas City Star*, July 31, 1923.

[30]*Tulsa Daily World*, July 1, 1923.
[31]*Ibid.*, July 2, 1923.
[32]*Kansas City Times*, July 4, 1923.
[33]*Tulsa Daily World*, January 21, 1924.
[34]*Ibid.*, January 29, 1924.
[35]*Daily Oklahoman*, August 15, 1924; *Tulsa Daily World*, October 19, 1924.
[36]*Bartlesville Morning Examiner*, April 19, 1925; Phillips Petroleum Company, Annual Report, December 31, 1924.

Chapter 6

[1]Phillips Petroleum Company, Annual Report, December 31, 1925, *LEP Collection; Fort Worth Star Telegram*, April 18, 1925.
[2]*National Magazine*, April 20, 1925, p. 519.
[3]*Fort Worth Star Telegram*, April 17, 18, 26, 1925; *Tulsa Tribune*, April 19, 1925; *Bartlesville Daily Enterprise*, April 20, 1925.
[4]Unidentified newsclipping, *LEP Collection*.
[5]*Bartlesville Morning Examiner*, November 13, 1925.
[6]*Amarillo Evening Post*, December 17, 1925; *Boston News Bureau*, April 13, 1926.
[7]*Bartlesville Morning Examiner*, March 3, 1926; April 18, 1926.
[8]*San Francisco Chronicle*, July 23, 1926.
[9]*Ibid.*, August 26, 1926.
[10]Phillips Petroleum Company, Annual Report, December 31, 1926, *LEP Collection; Bartlesville Morning Examiner*, March 3, 1927; Phillips Petroleum Company, Annual Meeting and Inspection, April 14-21, 1927, *LEP Collection; Kansas City Times*, May 25, 1927.
[11]A photostatic copy of the check was preserved by Phillips, clearly indicating his pleasure at the quick "turn around" in bond sales. *LEP Collection*.
[12]*Tulsa Daily World*, May 24, 1927; *Tulsa Tribune*, May 24, 1927; *Bartlesville Daily Enterprise*, May 23, 1927.
[13]*Daily Oklahoman*, May 24, 1927.
[14]*Bartlesville Morning Examiner*, May 24, 1927.
[15]*Amarillo Daily News*, October 18, 1927; *Tulsa Daily World*, October 18, 19, 1927.
[16]Franks, *The Oklahoma Petroleum Industry*, p. 120; *Wichita Eagle*, May 24, 1927.
[17]*Wichita Eagle*, May 24, 1927; *Daily Oklahoman*, June 3, 1927; *Bartlesville Morning Examiner*, July 23, 1927; Franks, *The Oklahoma Petroleum Industry*, p. 115.
[18]*Bartlesville Morning Examiner*, July 3, 1927.
[19]*Bartlesville Morning Examiner*, July 3, 31, 1927; *New York Times*, August 18, 1927.
[20]*Bartlesville Morning Examiner*, August 9, 1927; "Dole Prize Win-

ner Uses Natural Gasoline Fuel: Phillips Sponsor,"*Oil and Gas Journal*, August, 1927, p. 15.

21*Bartlesville Daily Enterprise*, August 17, 1927; *Bartlesville Morning Examiner*, August 18, 1927; *Chicago Herald Examiner*, August 18, 1927; *Tulsa Daily World*, August 18, 1927; *New York Times*, August 8, 1927; *Honolulu Star Bulletin*, August 17, 1927.

22*Bartlesville Morning Examiner*, August 19, 1927; *Bartlesville Daily Examiner*, August 19, 1927; *Tulsa Daily World*, August 18, 1927; *Honolulu Star Bulletin*, August 18, 1927.

23*Shield*, June, 1937, p. 25; unidentified newsclipping, *LEP Collection*. The clipping shows a picture of the craft which, though small, appeared to be an advancement in design.

24*Shield*, June, 1937, p. 28.

25*Amarillo Daily News*, October 11, 18, 1927.

26*Shield*, June, 1937, p. 28-29.

27*Omaha World-Herald*, May 26, 1928.

28*Des Moines Tribune*, March 27, 1929.

29*Bartlesville Daily Enterprise*, April 16, 1929; *Bartlesville Morning Examiner*, April 17, 1929.

30*Kansas City Star*, May 28, 1929; *Tulsa Tribune*, July 5, 1929; *Bartlesville Morning Examiner*, May 28, 1929, October 25, 1929.

31*Wall Street Journal*, October 30, 1929; *Bartlesville Morning Examiner*, October 25, 1929.

32*Bartlesville Morning Examiner*, November 1, 1929; *Tulsa Daily World*, November 3, 1929; *Arkansas City* (Kansas) *Daily Traveler*, November 7, 1929.

33*Wall Street Journal*, November 12, 1929; *Wall Street News*, November 12, 1929; *Minneapolis Evening Tribune*, December 17, 1929.

34*Des Moines Tribune*, November 6, 1929; *Des Moines Register*, November 6, 1929; *Minneapolis Evening Tribune*, December 17, 1929; *Omaha World Herald*, October 9, 29; *Omaha News*, October 9, 1929; *Washington Star*, December 15, 1929.

35*Bartlesville Morning Examiner*, February 8, 1930; *San Francisco Examiner*, February 14, 1930.

36*Bartlesville Morning Examiner*, June 5, 1930; *St. Louis Globe Democrat*, August 28, 1931; *St. Louis Post Dispatch*, August 2, 6, 19, 1931.

37The new additions were estimated to cost approximately $400,000. *Bartlesville Morning Examiner*, April 17, 1930.

38*Tulsa Tribune*, August 29, 1930; *San Diego* (California) *Sun*, August 30, 1930; *Daily Oklahoman*, August 30, 1930; *Las Vegas* (New Mexico) *Optic*, August 30, 1930.

39*Bartlesville Morning Examiner*, August 31, 1930; *Bartlesville Daily Enterprise*, August 30, 1930; *Trinidad* (Colorado) *Chronicle News*, August 30, 1930; *Colorado Springs Evening Telegram*, August 30, 1930; *Hartford* (Connecticut) *Times*, August 30, 1930.

40*Kansas City Journal*, August 30, 1930; *Joplin* (Missouri) *Globe*, August 30, 1930; *Des Moines Tribune-Capital*, August 30, 1930; *Tulsa Daily World*, August 30, 1930; *Kansas City Star*, August 30, 1930.

[41]*Kansas City Times*, August 30, 1930; *Knoxville* (Iowa) *Express*, September 4, 1930; *Fort Worth Star Telegram*, September 7, 1930.

[42]*Buffalo* (New York) *News*, September 2, 1930; *Tulsa Daily World*, August 30, 1930.

[43]*Kansas City Journal*, August 30, 1930; *Tulsa Tribune* (Extra), August 29, 1930; "Independent Merges with Phillips Company," *The Phillips Gas Tank*, September-October, 1930, p. 3; "Merger of Phillips and Independent," *Oil and Gas Journal*, September 4, 1930, p. 3.

[44]"Independent Merges with Phillips Company," *The Phillips Gas Tank*, September-October, 1930, p. 3.

[45]*New Orleans States*, September 15, 1930; *New Orleans Times Picayune*, September 16, 1930.

[46]*Kansas City Star*, September 12, 1930; *Bartlesville Daily Enterprise*, September 12, October 15, 1930; *Bartlesville Morning Examiner*, September 13, 29, 1930.

[47]*Bartlesville Morning Examiner*, October 19, 1930; *Springfield* (Illinois) *Daily News*, October 10, 1930.

[48]*Bartlesville Daily Enterprise*, March 20, 30; *The Phillips Gas Tank*, April, 1931, p. 5.

[49]*Wall Street Journal*, May 4, 1931.

[50]*Bartlesville Morning Examiner*, May 29, 1931.

[51]*Tulsa Daily World*, July 11, 1931; *Bartlesville Morning Examiner*, July 11, 1931.

[52]*Bartlesville Morning Examiner*, July 11, 1931.

[53]*Bartlesville Daily Enterprise*, July 28, 1931; Franks, *The Oklahoma Petroleum Industry*, p. 148.

[54]*Bartlesville Daily Enterprise*, August 5, 1931; *Bartlesville Morning Examiner*, August 13, 16, 1931.

[55]*Bartlesville Morning Examiner*, August 12, 25, 1931; Franks, *Oklahoma Petroleum Industry*, p. 166; *Tulsa Tribune*, August 23, 1931.

[56]*Bartlesville Morning Examiner*, August 23, 28, 1931; *Bartlesville Daily Enterprise*, August 24, 1931; *Tulsa Daily World*, August 23, 24, 1931; *Kansas City Star*, August 23, 1931.

[57]*Bedford* (Iowa) *Free Press*, October 22, 1931; *Oklahoma City Times*, November 4, 1931; *Bartlesville Morning Examiner*, November 2, 1931.

[58]*Bartlesville Morning Examiner*, December 22, 1931.

[59]Interview, Ms. Dorothy Saunders with author, July 28, 1980, *OHAA*.

[60]*Wichita Beacon*, January 10, 1932; *Bartlesville Morning Examiner*, March 18, 1932; April 20, 1932; *Bartlesville Daily Enterprise*, April 20, 1932.

[61]*Omaha World-Herald*, May 1, 1932.

[62]*Battle Creek Sanitarium News*, September 9, 1932; *Battle Creek Morning Journal*, October 10, 1932.

[63]*Minneapolis Evening Tribune*, October 24, 1932; *Des Moines Tribune*, October 28, 1932; *Phillips Gas Tank*, November 21, 1932, p. 2.

[64]H. H. McClintock to L. E. Phillips, December 25, 1932, *LEP Collection*.

⁶⁵*Miami Daily News*, February 19, 1933.

⁶⁶*Des Moines Tribune*, June 6, 1933; *Wichita Eagle*, October 15, 1933; *Dodge City Globe*, October 15, 1933.

⁶⁷H. H. McClintock to L. E. Phillips, November 11, 1933, *LEP Collection.*

⁶⁸L. E. Phillips to Heinrich Hagenbeck, January 9, 1934, *LEP Collection.*

Chapter 7

¹Interview, Philip Rex Phillips with author, July 10, 1980, *OHAA.*

²An excellent summary of his philosophy can be found in *Bartlesville Daily Enterprise*, December 5, 1925; see also *Oklahoma City News*, September 7, 1940.

³*Bartlesville Daily Enterprise*, April 20, 1926. The news article quoted an earlier edition of the *Bartlesville Daily Enterprise*, June 3, 1904.

⁴*Bartlesville Morning Examiner*, June 18, 1906; *Bartlesville Daily Enterprise*, June 20, 1906.

⁵*Bartlesville Daily Enterprise*, June 28, 1906; July 2, 1906; unidentified newsclipping, *LEP Collection.*

⁶*Bartlesville Daily Enterprise*, January 9, 1907; *Bartlesville News*, January 9, 10, 1907.

⁷*Bartlesville Daily Enterprise*, undated newsclipping, *LEP Collection.*

⁸*Bartlesville Daily Enterprise*, February 26, 28, 1907; March 1, 1907.

⁹*Ibid.*, April 13, 1908; June 8, 1908.

¹⁰Bartlesville Commercial Club, Second Annual Booster Banquet, February 28, 1909, program copy, *LEP Collection; Bartlesville Morning Examiner*, March 22, 23, 1910; *Bartlesville Daily Enterprise*, March 22, 1910.

¹¹*Bartlesville Daily Enterprise*, March 20, 30, 1911; April 1, 1911; October 22, 1911; November 30, 1911.

¹²Unidentified newsclipping, *LEP Collection.*

¹³*Bartlesville Daily Enterprise*, March 30, 1917; April 7, 1917; *Daily Oklahoman*, April 11, 19, 1917.

¹⁴*Bartlesville Daily Enterprise*, June 16, 1917.

¹⁵*Bartlesville Morning Examiner*, June 15, 19, 1917.

¹⁶*Daily Oklahoman*, November 24, 1917; *Bartlesville Daily Enterprise*, November 27, 1917.

¹⁷*Ardmore* (Oklahoma) *News*, December 6, 1917.

¹⁸*Daily Oklahoman*, December 23, 25, 1917; *Oklahoma City News*, December 24, 1917; Henry P. Davison to L. E. Phillips, December 28, 1917, *LEP Collection.*

¹⁹*Bartlesville Morning Examiner*, January 14, 1918; *Oklahoma City Times*, April 10, 16, 1918.

²⁰*Daily Oklahoman*, April 15, 18, 1918; May 4, 1918; *Oklahoma City News*, April 17, 1918.

²¹*Oklahoma City Times*, May 14, 1918; *Bartlesville Morning Examiner*, May 18, 1918.

²²*Oklahoma City News*, May 17, 1918.

²³*Oklahoma City Times*, May 15, 1918; *Daily Oklahoman*, May 28, 1918.

²⁴*Oklahoma City News*, May 28, 1918; *Daily Oklahoman*, May 28, 1918; *Sooners in the War*, September 23, 1918.

²⁵*Daily Oklahoman*, August 31, 1918.

²⁶*Oklahoma City Times*, September 25, 1918; *Daily Oklahoman*, October 6, 1918; *Okmulgee* (Oklahoma) *Daily*, October 2, 1918.

²⁷*Daily Oklahoman*, October 11, 13, 19, 1918; *Oklahoma City News*, October 12, 19, 1918; *Oklahoma City Times*, October 11, 1918.

²⁹*Daily Oklahoman*, October 19, 1918.

³⁰*Bartlesville Morning Examiner*, November 24, 1918.

³¹*Daily Oklahoman*, December 1, 1918; *Frederick* (Oklahoma) *Leader*, November 28, 1918; *Anadarko* (Oklahoma) *American-Democrat*, December 5, 1918.

³²*Daily Oklahoman*, December 22, 1918.

³³*Ibid.*, January 5, 1918.

³⁴*Ibid.*

³⁵*Christian Echo* (First Christian Church, Bartlesville), May 2, 1929, *LEP Collection*.

Chapter 8

¹*Topeka Capital*, December 7, 8, 1939; *Topeka Journal*, December 7, 1939.

²Frank Phillips to L. E. Phillips, May 16, 1935; Phillips Petroleum Company, Board Resolution, April 24, 1934, *LEP Collection*.

³*Wichita Beacon*, July 4, 1934; *Bartlesville Morning Examiner*, November 1, 1935.

⁴*Standard Poland News*, January, 1940.

⁵*Bartlesville Morning Examiner*, September 5, 1940; October 26, 1940; *Bartlesville Daily Enterprise*, October 30, 1940.

⁶*Tulsa Tribune*, November 3, 1934.

⁷*Lincoln* (Nebraska) *State Journal*, November 7, 1934; *Denver Post*, July 21, 1940; *Kansas City Times*, June 14, 1935.

⁸*Fargo* (North Dakota) *Forum*, January 13, 1936; *Minneapolis Journal*, January 16, 1936; *Oil and Gas Journal*, January 23, 1936, p. 93; *San Francisco Chronicle*, August 15, 1941.

⁹*Kansas City Star*, December 14, 16, 1934; unidentified newsclipping, *LEP Collection*.

¹⁰*The McGuffevite*, II, No. 9 (May, 1925); unidentified newsclipping, *LEP Collection*.

¹¹*Charlottetown* (Canada) *Guardian*, July 29, 1935; *St. John* (Canada) *Telegraph Journal*, August 8, 1935.

¹²*Kansas City Star*, November 25, 30, 1936; *Jacksonville* (Florida)

Times, December 5, 1936; *New Orleans Times Picayune*, December 1, 1936; *Bartlesville Morning Examiner*, December 8, 1936.

[13]*New Orleans States*, December 1, 2, 1936.

[14]*Clearwater* (Florida) *Sun*, March 6, 11, 1938; *Dunedin* (Florida) *Times*, March 11, 1938; *St. Petersburg* (Florida) *Times*, March 11, 1938; *Ogden* (Utah) *Tribune*, August 6, 1939.

[15]Phillips was an avid photographer. The photographs he took on the trips here mentioned are arranged chronologically with annotations in the several photograph albums, *LEP Collection*.

[16]This is a pencil copy of an original communication which he wrote as a "club letter" to members of the Anchor Club on June 25, 1928, and is to be found in *The Anchor Club*, photograph album, *LEP Collection*.

[17]The interview was printed in the *Boston Commercial*, November 26, 1921.

[18]Photograph Albums, *LEP Collection; Oklahoma Banker*, October, 1921, p. 12; October, 1922, p. 13.

[19]Manuel Quezon to L. E. Phillips, December 24, 1941, *LEP Collection; Bartlesville Morning Examiner*, January 1, 1942.

[20]*Fort Worth Star Telegram*, December 24, 1926; Amon Carter to L. E. Phillips, December 23, 1926, *LEP Collection*; L. E. Phillips to Amon Carter, *LEP Collection*.

[21]Irving S. Cobb to L. E. Phillips, December 6, 1941; L. E. Phillips to Irving S. Cobb, December 2, 1941; Irving S. Cobb to L. E. Phillips, December 12, 1941, *LEP Collection*.

[22]*New York Herald Tribune*, August 17, 1935; *Bartlesville Daily Enterprise*, August 16, 1935; *New York Times*, August 17, 1935.

[23]Interview, Philip Rex Phillips with author, July 10, 1980, *OHAA*.

[24]Will Rogers to L. E. Phillips, January 1, 1935, *LEP Collection*; *Bartlesville Daily Examiner*, December 15, 20, 1934; *Kansas City Star*, December 24, 1934.

[25]*Kansas City Star*, July 26, 1935.

[26]L. E. Phillips to Will Rogers, August 10, 1935, telegram in *LEP Collection*.

[27]*New York World Telegram*, August 17, 1935.

[28]*Berkshire* (Massachusetts) *Courier*, August 22, 1935; L. E. Phillips to Mrs. Will Rogers, August 16, 1935, copy of telegram in *LEP Collection*.

[29]Photograph Albums, *LEP Collection*.

[30]*Creston* (Iowa) *News Advertiser*, September 20, 1941.

[31]The narrative describing the Anchor Club is drawn from: *Omaha Evening World*, December 11, 1925; *Bedford* (Iowa) *Times Republican*, October 21, 1926; December 11, 1930; *Excelsior Springs* (Missouri) *Daily Standard*, November 25, 1928; *Des Moines Tribune-Capital*, November 29, 1928; *Bartlesville Morning Examiner*, November 7, 11, 1937; *Denver Post*, August 31, 1935.

[32]*Excelsior Springs* (Missouri) *Daily Standard*, November 25, 1928.

[33]Phillips was declining an invitation to attend a Bartlesville

Chamber of Commerce dinner in honor of Frank Phillips. L. E. Phillips to John Cronin, May 2, 1942, pencil copy of telegran in *LEP Collection*; H. H. McClintock to L. E. Phillips, December 25, 1940, *LEP Collection*.

[34]The numerous messages of encouragement and concern are in the *LEP Collection*.

[35]Phil Starr to L. E. Phillips, August 16, 1943, *LEP Collection*.

Chapter 9

[1]L. E. Phillips to Kenneth S. Adams, December 26, 1940, *LEP Collection*.

[2]Kenneth S. Adams to L. E. Phillips, December 28, 1940, *LEP Collection*.

[3]*Los Angeles Express and Herald*, January 9, 1941; *Los Angeles Times*, January 10, 1941; *Bartlesville Morning Examiner*, January 12, 1941; *Bartlesville Daily Enterprise*, February 14, 1941.

[4]*The Poland China Journal*, June, 1941, pp. 10-11.

[5]*Bartlesville Morning Examiner*, March 7, 9, 1941; April 18, 27, 1941; *Washington* (Oklahoma) *Countian*, July 1, 1941.

[6]*Bartlesville Daily Enterprise*, June 22, 1941; *Bartlesville Morning Examiner*, September 9, 12, 1941.

[7]*San Francisco Chronicle*, August 15, 1941; *Creston* (Iowa) *News*, September 20, 1941.

[8]*Oklahoma Banker*, May, 1942, p. 11; *Bartlesville Morning Examiner*, May 27, 1942; *Tulsa Tribune*, May 27, 1942.

[9]*Philnews*, June, 1942, p. 6.

[10]*Ibid*, p. 7; July, 1942, p. 4; *Borger* (Texas) *Daily Herald*, June 14, 1942; *Tulsa Daily World*, June 12, 1942.

[11]*Bartlesville Morning Examiner*, June 13, 1942.

[12]*Bartlesville Examiner*, May 27, 1942; *Philnews*, July, 1942, p. 4.

[13]Philip Rex Phillips to L. E. Phillips, telegram dated July 31, 1942, *LEP Collection*. *Bartlesville Morning Examiner*, August 1, 1942; *The Independent* (Kansas City Journal of Society), November 27, 1943, *LEP Collection*; interview, Ms. Dorothy Saunders with author, July 28, 1980, *OHAA*.

[14]*Kansas City Star*, October 16, 1942.

[15]*Bartlesville Daily Enterprise*, December 24, 1942; unidentified newsclipping, *LEP Collection*; *Tulsa Daily World*, February 17, 1943; *Washington* (Oklahoma) *Countian*, June 1, 1943.

[16]*Bartlesville Morning Examiner*, June 28, 1943.

[17]Interview, Ms. Dorothy Saunders with author, July 28, 1980, *OHAA*.

[18]*Ibid*,; interview, Philip Rex Phillips with author, July 10, 1980, *OHAA*.

[19]L. E. Phillips to Lenora Phillips, April 28, 1915, *LEP Collection*:

[20]L. E. Phillips to Lenora Phillips, flower card, November 26, 1941, *LEP Collection.*

[21]Interview, Ms. Dorothy Saunders with author, July 28, 1980, *OHAA.*

[22]E. G. Bennett to L. E. Phillips, September 14, 1943; George B. Rex to L. E. Phillips, August 23, 1943; Guy Liggett, September 4, 1943; all letters in *LEP Collection.*

[23]*Bartlesville Daily Enterprise,* October 10, 1943; Minutes, 53rd Annual Meeting, Anchor Club, October 8-10, 1943, *LEP Collection.*

[24]Interview, Ms. Dorothy Saunders with author, July 28, 1980, *OHAA.*

[25]News releases from cities all over the United States, telling of his death, are contained in the *LEP Collection.*

[26]The numerous expressions of sympathy have been preserved in the *LEP Collection.*

[27]*Guthrie* (Oklahoma) *Leader,* April 17, 1944.

[28]*St. Joseph* (Missouri) *Gazette,* April 17, 1944.

[29]*Tulsa Tribune,* April 19, 1944.

[30]*Washington* (Oklahoma) *Countian,* April 18, 1944.

[31]*Tulsa Daily World,* April 18, 1944.

[32]*Olathe* (Kansas) *Democrat,* April 20, 1944.

[33]*Bartlesville Daily Enterprise,* April 17, 1944.

[34]Amon Carter to Mrs. L. E. Phillips, April 28, 1944, *LEP Collection.*

[35]Victoria McDougal Heller to Mrs. L. E. Phillips, April 17, 1944, *LEP Collection.*

[36]*Bartlesville Daily Enterprise,* April 17, 1944; Harry L. Ice to Mrs. L. E. Phillips, April 20, 1944, *LEP Collection.* Reverend Ice sent a copy of his sermon to Lenora with the letter cited.

[37]L. E. Phillips to Kenneth S. Adams, December 26, 1940, *LEP Collection.*

BIBLIOGRAPHY

Primary Sources

A.   Lee Eldas Phillips Collection

Currently in possession of Philip Rex Phillips, Bartlesville, Oklahoma. The collection consists of autobiographical notes, genealogies, letters, newspaper clippings, memorabilia, and photographs compiled almost exclusively by Lee Eldas Phillips from 1890-1943. Items related to his death and the period of post interment were compiled by his wife, Mrs. Lenora Phillips, and his eldest son, Philip Rex Phillips.

B.   Newspapers

Amarillo (Texas) *Daily News*, 1927.
Amarillo (Texas) *Evening Post*, 1925.
Anadarko (Oklahoma) *American-Democrat*, 1918.
Ardmore (Oklahoma) *News*, 1917.
Arkansas City (Kansas) *Daily Traveler*, 1929.
Bartlesville (Oklahoma) *Daily Enterprise*, 1908-1944.
Bartlesville (Oklahoma) *Morning Examiner*, 1905-1944.
Bartlesville (Oklahoma) *News*, 1907.
Battle Creek (Michigan) *Morning Journal*, 1932.
Battle Creek (Michigan) *Sanitarium News*, 1932.
Bedford (Iowa) *Free Press*, 1931.
Bedford (Iowa) *Times Republican*, 1926.
Berkshire (Massachusetts) *Courier*, 1935.
Borger (Texas) *Daily Herald*, 1942.
Boston (Massachusetts) *Commercial*, 1921.
Boston (Massachusetts) *News Bureau*, 1926.
Buffalo (New York) *News*, 1930.
Charlottetown (New Brunswick, Canada) *Guardian*, 1935.
Chicago (Illinois) *Herald Examiner*, 1927.
Clearwater (Florida) *Sun*, 1938.
Colorado Springs (Colorado) *Evening Telegram*, 1930.
Conway (Iowa) *Journal*, 1898, 1901.
Creston (Iowa) *Daily Advertiser*, 1902, 1903.
Creston (Iowa) *Daily Examiner*, 1902

Creston (Iowa) *Morning American*, 1899, 1902.
Creston (Iowa) *News Advertiser*, 1941.
Daily Oklahoman (Oklahoma City, Oklahoma) 1914-1930.
Denver (Colorado) *Post*, 1930, 1935, 1940.
Des Moines (Iowa) *Register*, 1929.
Des Moines (Iowa) *Tribune-Capital*, 1928-1933.
Dodge City (Kansas) *Globe*, 1933.
Dunedin (Florida) *Times*, 1938.
Excelsior Springs (Missouri) *Daily Standard*, 1928.
Fargo (North Dakota) *Forum*, 1936.
Fort Worth (Texas) *Star Telegram*, 1925, 1926, 1930.
Frederick (Oklahoma) *Leader*, 1918.
Gravity (Iowa) *Republican*, 1917.
Guthrie (Oklahoma) *Leader*, 1944.
Hartford (Connecticut) *Times*, 1930.
Honolulu (Hawaii) *Star Bulletin*, 1927.
Jacksonville (Florida) *Times*, 1936.
Joplin (Missouri) *Globe*, 1930.
Kansas City (Missouri) *Journal*, 1930.
Kansas City (Missouri) *Post*, 1914.
Kansas City (Missouri) *Star*, 1923-1942.
Kansas City (Missouri) *Times*, 1922-1935.
Knoxville (Iowa) *Express*, 1930.
Knoxville (Iowa) *Journal*, 1905.
Las Vegas (New Mexico) *Optic*, 1930.
Lincoln (Nebraska) *State Journal*, 1934.
Los Angeles (California) *Express and Herald*, 1941.
Los Angeles (California) *Times*, 1941.
McGuffeyite, 1925.
Miami (Florida) *Daily News*, 1933.
Minneapolis (Minnesota) *Evening Tribune*, 1929, 1932.
Minneapolis (Minnesota) *Journal*, 1936.
Nautilus (Bartlesville High School), 1923, 1924.
New Orleans (Louisiana) *States*, 1930, 1936.
New Orleans (Louisiana) *Times Picayune*, 1930, 1936.
New State Tribune (Oklahoma), 1911.
New York Herald Tribune, 1935.
New York Times, 1927.
New York World Telegram, 1935.
Ogden (Utah) *Tribune*, 1939.
Oklahoma City (Oklahoma) *News*, 1917, 1918, 1940.
Oklahoma City (Oklahoma) *Times*, 1918, 1922, 1931.
Okmulgee (Oklahoma) *Daily*, 1918.
Olathe (Kansas) *Democrat*, 1944.
Omaha (Nebraska) *News*, 1929.
Omaha (Nebraska) *World-Herald*, 1925, 1928, 1929, 1932.
Pawhuska (Oklahoma) *Daily Capital*, 1922.
Rocky Mountain News (Denver, Colorado), 1929.

St. Joseph (Missouri) *Gazette*, 1944.
St. John (New Brunswick, Canada) *Telegraph Journal*, 1935.
St. Louis (Missouri) *Globe Democrat*, 1931.
St. Louis (Missouri) *Post Dispatch*, 1931.
St. Petersburg (Florida) *Times*, 1938.
San Diego (California) *Sun*, 1930.
San Francisco (California) *Chronicle*, 1926, 1941.
San Francisco (California) *Examiner*, 1930.
Sooners in the War (Oklahoma), 1918.
Springfield (Illinois) *Daily News*, 1930.
Topeka (Kansas) *Capital*, 1939.
Topeka (Kansas) *Journal*, 1939.
Trinidad (Colorado) *Chronicle News*, 1930.
Tulsa (Oklahoma) *Daily World*, 1919-1944.
Tulsa (Oklahoma) *Tribune*, 1921-1944.
Wall Street News (New York, New York), 1929.
Wall Street Journal (New York, New York), 1929, 1931.
The Washington Countian (Bartlesville, Oklahoma), 1941, 1943, 1944.
Washington (D. C.) *Star*, 1929.
Wichita (Kansas) *Beacon*, 1929, 1932, 1934.
Wichita (Kansas) *Eagle*, 1927, 1929, 1933.

C. Interviews

Billbe, Glenroy, with author, September 29, 1980.
Cummings, Charles, with author, October 15, 1980.
Endacott, Paul, with author, July 28, 1980.
Fitzgarrald, L. E., with author, September 29, 1980.
Phillips, Philip Rex, with author, July 10, 1980.
Phillips, Philip Rex, with Jimmy M. Skaggs, March 16, 1979; original in Phillips Petroleum Company Archives.
Saunders, Dorothy, with author, July 28, 1980.

Published Materials

"An Appreciation." *The Christian Echo* (Bartlesville), December 9, 1926, p. 1.
"Anna Anderson Davis." *Shield*, Vol. 4, No. 4 (Fourth Quarter, 1979), p. 6.
"Auspicious Opening of Liberty Central Trust Company, St. Louis." *Trans-Mississippi Banker*, February, 1921, p. 9.
"Bankers Who Made History." *Coast Banker*, November, 1921, p. 18.
Barringer, E. L. "North Dakota and Minnesota Jobbers to Attend Oil Code Conference." *National Petroleum News*, January 22, 1936, p. 11.

Berger, Bill D., and Kenneth E. Anderson. *Modern Petroleum: A Basic Primer of the Industry.* Tulsa: The Petroleum Publishing Company, 1978.

"A Billion Dollar Dinner." *The Oil Trade*, January, 1925, p. 20.

"A Bird's Eye View." *Shield*, June, 1937, p. 5.

Clark, J. Stanley. *The Oil Industry: From the Drake Well to the Conservation Era.* Norman: University of Oklahoma Press, 1958.

Clark, James A. *The Chronological History of the Petroleum and Natural Gas Industries.* Houston: Clark Book Company, 1963.

"Everybody Enjoyed Themselves." *The Christian Echo* (Bartlesville), June 13, 1929, p. 1.

"Famous Red Cross Slogan a Banker's Idea." *Mid-Continent Banker*, March, 1919, pp. 8-9.

"Finished." *The Christian Echo* (Bartlesville), January 1, 1925, p. 1.

Forbes, Gerald. "History of the Osage Blanket Lease." *Chronicles of Oklahoma*, Vol. 19, No. 1 (March, 1941), pp. 70-81.

"The Fourth Liberty Loan." *The Employer*, September, 1918, cover.

Franks, Kenny. *The Oklahoma Petroleum Industry.* Norman: University of Oklahoma Press, 1980.

Glasscock, Carl B. *Then Came Oil: The Story of the Last Frontier.* New York: Bobbs-Merrill, 1938.

"The Glorious Red Cross Work." *The Investor*, December, 1917, p. 7.

Gregory, Robert. *Oil in Oklahoma.* Muskogee: Leake Industries Inc., 1976.

"If We Hadn't Hit the Anna, We'd Have been Back in Iowa." *Shield*, Vol. 4, No. 4 (Fourth Quarter, 1979), pp. 2-5.

"Independent Merges with Phillips Company." *Phillips Gas Tank*, September-October, 1930, p. 3.

Ironside, Roberta. *An Adventure Called Skelly: A History of Skelly Oil Company Through Fifty Years, 1919-1969.* New York: Appleton-Century-Crofts, 1970.

Killian, D. P. "Henry Vernon Foster, 1875-1939." *Chronicles of Oklahoma*, Vol. 20, No. 4 (December, 1942), pp. 441-43.

King, O. W. "The Phillips Petroleum Company." *Phillips Gas Tank*, September 10, 1928, pp. 1, 3.

"L. E. Phillips, Director, Federal Reserve Bank, Tenth District." *Oklahoma Banker*, December, 1926, cover, p. 28.

"L. E. Phillips: Our Vice President." *Better Service*, March 18, 1920, p. 4.

"L. E. Phillips Would Popularize 'See America First' Slogan." *Phillips Gas Tank*, April, 1931, p. 5.

"Leaders in Oil Industry." *Oil and Gas Journal*, October 1, 1925, p. A60.

"Lieutenant John Wilbur Starr, U.S.N.R." *The Independent: Kansas City's Weekly Journal of Society*, Vol. 80, No. 47 (November 27, 43), p. 1.

Lobsenz, Norman M. *The Boots Adams Story*. Bartlesville: Phillips Petroleum Company, 1965.

"Marketing." *Shield*, June, 1937, pp. 28-29.

Mathews, John Joseph. *Life and Death of an Oilman: The Career of E. W. Marland*. Norman: University of Oklahoma Press, 1951.

"Merger of Phillips and Independent." *Oil and Gas Journal*, September 15, 1930, pp. 40, 78.

"Methods of Cementing Deep Oil Wells." *The Oil Weekly*, December 26, 1924, pp. 27-28.

"Mr. and Mrs. Phillips Visit Mission Station." *The Christian Echo* (Bartlesville), January 22, 1930, p. 2.

["News Note: L. E. Phillips"]. *Southwestern Banker*, October, 1914.

"1903: Oil Boom." *Philnews* (Special Edition), November 28, 1939.

"Northeast Oklahoma Hereford Breeders Organize." *The Ranchman*, December, 1942, p. 9.

"Personal Mention: Men You Know." *The Oil Weekly*, February 11, 1927, p. 64.

Phillips, L. E. "The Bank Guaranty Law." *Commercial West*, July 11, 1914, p. 4.

———. "The Guaranty Law." *North Dakota Banker*, January, 1918, pp. 31-38.

———. "Lest We Forget." *Oklahoma Banker*, December, 1934, cover.

———. "Our Taxation System." *Oklahoma Banker*, April, 1917, pp. 10-11.

———. "Practical Tests of Education." University of Tulsa *Bulletin*, Vol. 36, No. 7 (July, 1929), pp. 1-7.

———. "The Responsibility of the Trained Mind." *Phillips Crusader* (Enid, Oklahoma), Vol. 7, No. 4 (July 15, 1931), pp. 1-4.

"The Phillips of Bartlesville." *National Elks Horn*, October, 1930, p. 8.

"Phillips 'Pete' Adventures in Chemistry." *Business Week*, December 31, 1949, pp. 22-24.

"Phillips Petroleum Company." *The Bridgeport Driller*, Vol. 7, No. 10 (October, 1930), pp. 3-5.

"Phillips Petroleum: 25 Years of Progress." *World Petroleum*, June, 1942, pp. 25-45.

"Philson Farm Adds More Good Ones." *Standard Poland China News*, November, 1940, p. 6.

"Philson Farms Will Show." *Standard Poland China News*, July, 1940, p. 5.

"Prominent Oil Men." *Oil and Gas Journal*, October 4, 1921, p. R-6.

"Quarter-Century Employees to Be Honored." *Philnews*, June, 1942, pp. 6-7.

Rister, Carl Coke. *Oil! Titan of the Southwest*. Norman: University of Oklahoma Press, 1949.

Sinclair Oil and Gas Company. *A Great Name in Oil: Sinclair Through Fifty Years.* New York: McGraw-Hill, 1966.

Smallwood, James M. *An Oklahoma Adventure: Of Banks and Bankers.* Oklahoma City: Oklahoma Heritage Association, 1979.

Smith, Lawrence E. "Oil Company Executive is Elected to Federal Reserve Board." *National Petroleum News,* December 1, 1926, pp. 8-9.

Teague, Margaret W. *History of Washington County and Surrounding Area.* 2 Vols. Bartlesville: Bartlesville Historical Commission, 1968.

"Tenth Federal Reserve in Exceptional Position." *Oklahoma Banker,* October, 1930, p. 23.

"A Tour of the Mid-Continent Oil Fields." *National Magazine,* April 20, 1925, pp. 519-524.

"Tulsa Oil Show Success." *The Bridgeport Driller,* Vol. 7, No. 10 (October, 1930), p. 12.

"25 Years of Service." *Philnews,* July, 1942, pp. 4-5.

"The 26th Annual Convention of the Oklahoma Bankers Association." *Oklahoma Banker,* June, 1922, p. 13.

"Two Tracts Break Previous Records For Osage County Acreage." *National Petroleum News,* March 8, 1922, p. 25.

Tyson, Carl N., James H. Thomas, and Odie B. Faulk. *The McMan: The Lives of Robert M. McFarland and James A. Chapman.* Oklahoma City: Oklahoma Heritage Association, 1977.

"A Unique Organization." *The Midwestern* (Des Moines, Iowa), February, 1910, p. 12.

Walker, C. H. "Philson Farms Combines Beauty and Utility." *The Poland China Journal,* June, 1941, pp. 10-11.

Washington County Historical Society. *A Pictoral History of Bartlesville.* Bartlesville: Washington County Historican Society, Inc., 1972.

"What They Said of Kansas City." *The Western Financier,* September, 1916, p. 1.

"Wichita Becomes Manufacturing Center." *The Wichita* (Chamber of Commerce), Vol. 4, No. 6 (June, 1927), pp. 1, 11.

Williams, Joe. *Bartlesville: Remembrances of Times Past, Reflections of Today.* Bartlesville: TRW Reda Pump Division, 1979.

Williamson, Harold F., Arnold R. Daum, Ralph L. Andreano, and Gilbert C. Klose. *The American Petroleum Industry.* 2 Vols. Evanston: Northwestern University Press, 1959, 1963.

INDEX